OUTLET GUIDE:
Midwest

Illinois, Indiana, Iowa, Michigan
Minnesota, Missouri, Ohio, Wisconsin

by A. Tightwad and A. Pennypincher

A Voyager Book

The Globe Pequot Press

Old Saybrook, Connecticut

Library of Congress Cataloging-in-Publication Data

Tightwad, A.
    Outlet guide: Midwest : Illinois, Indiana, Iowa, Michigan, Minnesota, Missouri, Ohio, Wisconsin / by A. Tightwad & A. Pennypincher. — 2nd ed.
        p. cm.
    Rev. ed. of : Factory outlet guide to the Midwest. 1st ed. 1991.
    "A Voyager book"
    Includes index.
    ISBN 1-56440-238-X
    1. Outlet stores—Middle West—Directories. I. Pennypincher, A.
    II. Tightwad, A. Factory outlet guide to the Midwest. III. Title.
    HF5429.215.U6T54 1993
    381'.15'02577—dc20   93-1581
                                                                 CIP

Manufactured in the United States of America
Second Edition/First Printing

Contents

Introduction

Why do outlet stores exist? Outlets are the manufacturers' solution to selling goods that tie up precious money. Some manufacturers find it too costly to send a quality item back through the production line because it's missing a button or to let last year's overproduced style gather dust in the warehouse. And then there are the headaches that manufacturers encounter from ever-larger department store chains that cancel orders, return unsold goods, or carry private label goods. So the manufacturers send all this merchandise to an outlet store, where it is labeled as first-quality overruns, seconds, irregulars, or damaged.

Factories in major Midwest cities and other manufacturing centers started the outlet concept years ago. Opening spartan stores, usually adjoining their plants, they offered defective but usable goods and excess merchandise. Their employees and sometimes the neighborhood general public had access to the items and snapped up these bargains. The news spread by word of mouth to frugal farmers and cost-conscious city dwellers, who were eager to save their hard-earned dollars. Manufacturers spruced up sales areas and started to advertise, and factory outlets slowly became a part of the shopping scene.

The next step in this evolution was the appearance of factory outlet centers, a group of outlet stores located close to each other. Originally an East Coast phenomenon, the first outlet center opened nearly fifteen years ago in Reading, Pennsylvania, now cited as the birthplace of factory outlet shopping. Consumers looking for bargains flocked to these centers by the busload.

The success of these centers resulted in the development of well-planned outlet malls. Their attraction is plenty of parking, easy accessibility, and a variety of stores. Offering savings from 20 to 75 percent, factory outlet malls are fast becoming bargain-hunting meccas, as their assortment of goods ranges from shelves to shoes and then some. This one-stop-shopping convenience trend has become so popular that across the country there are more than 300 outlet chains with more than 6,000 store locations.

In the land-rich Midwest, outlet malls have been cropping up in less-populated areas along the interstates and tourist spots, so placed to avoid competing with department stores that offer merchandise at retail prices. In fact since the first edition of this book, nearly ten outlet malls have been added to the guide and additional outlet malls are planned for the near future.

Individual factory outlets, in contrast, tend to remain in larger cities, the older established centers of commerce. Many are still adjacent to the factory or located as freestanding units. Although not as sleek or as attractively decorated as their mall counterparts, they should in no way be overlooked. Low overhead and low-tech merchandising translates into large discounts.

Don't assume outlet merchandise is low quality or undesirable. Granted, whether shopping at an outlet mall or single outlet, you will find some defective merchandise. But many quality items come from prestigious companies that manufacture well-recognized brand names, and discerning shoppers can separate the wheat from the chaff and come away with great bargains. The bottom line is that outlet merchandise can cost half the retail price.

Just like retail stores, some outlets run annual, clearance, or seasonal sales. An item that may be a good buy at the discounted price then becomes a great buy. Check with your favorite outlets to see if you can tap into this extra bargain bounty. Some outlets may distribute flyers to advertise sales and special events. Stop by the mall office to check if a mailing list is compiled and add your name to the list. (Regular annual sales at specific outlets are noted in the geographic portion of the book, under the "additional savings" heading. Other outlets may have sales during the year, but if they are not annual events, they are not listed.)

Who shops at outlet stores? You'd be surprised! Some people simply love to bargain shop. Others just can't stand paying full retail price. A third group—some senior citizens, single mothers, or lower-income people—can't afford to purchase full-price goods. At some point it seems nearly all of us need to arm ourselves in the battle of the budget. By shopping at outlets, the cost of this book can be saved almost instantly. Realistically it is possible to save 50 percent of your shopping budget.

Even though this book focuses primarily on outlet shopping, a small number of select stores that offer deep discounts are also provided as a reader service. Deep discounters are middlemen who buy merchandise from manufacturers or distributors and then mark it up for resale. Also known as "off-price" stores, they sell for less because their merchandise consists mostly of large-lot buys from manufacturers who need to sell quickly. Some stores that call themselves outlets are in reality "off-price" retailers. Although not true outlets, discounters need not be overlooked if you like their merchandise and prices. After all, our goal is saving money.

One final point: Outlets don't order merchandise in specific styles and sizes; they get what manufacturers can't sell through retail stores. The stock differs from day to day. Keep this in mind: If you see it and like it, buy it. The sweater or bedspread that catches your eye today probably won't be there tomorrow.

Planning Your Shopping Trip

Outlet shopping is more productive and less stressful when a few simple guidelines are followed.

Organize yourself before a shopping expedition by setting up a loose-leaf notebook. Establish an index listing birthdays, anniversaries, and other significant dates for friends and family members. Divide the notebook into sections. Set aside a section for each person for whom you shop. In each section, note the person's sizes for various goods, merchandise needed, color preference, favorite brand names, and desires. A home section, with room-by-room measurements, prepares you to take advantage of houseware bargains. Keep extra pages in the binder for categories as the need arises. With this information at your fingertips, your shopping expeditions can proceed smoothly.

Jot down prices when shopping at local retail stores. This establishes a retail price comparison so that you can judge the true outlet "deals." It also gives you an idea of current styles and colors.

Keep the *Outlet Guide: Midwest* in the car when driving to vacation destinations. Check the book or signs posted on the highway to see if you'll be passing near any outlet malls or stores. Refer to the Profiles section of this book to see if a detour is worth your while. A well-planned itinerary or unexpected detour can lead you to tremendous savings and help defray the cost of your trip.

To keep your budget-conscious life-style going strong even while on vacation, a list of state tourism contacts is included, along with toll-free phone numbers to maximize every savings opportunity. On The Go Publishing offers a list of more than 200 city, state, and regional/provincial tourism offices throughout North America, with toll-free phone numbers when available. For a copy send $3.00 plus a self-addressed, stamped, legal-size envelope to: P.O. Box 091033, Columbus, OH 43209. State tourism information centers are a valuable source of cost-saving information. You'll be made aware of less costly overnight accommodations, special discount packages, and reasonably priced restaurants. This translates into more money for shopping. When contacting these agencies, ask for updated outlet information in the area you plan to visit.

Using This Book

To simplify the use of this book, we have divided it into two sections:

1. The Profiles section includes generic information about each outlet in the book. Because outlets may vary somewhat from one location to another, we have listed name variations in this section to minimize any confusion.

2. Cities are listed in alphabetical order under their appropriate states in the geographic section. Individual outlets and malls are then listed alphabetically under cities. A basic map introducing each state's listings illustrates, in a general way, the location of cities covered in the text.

In compiling data for the book, every attempt to provide accurate information was made. Nevertheless, stores go out of business, they close for vacation, they change business hours, and they move. There is no way to control or predict the ebb and flow of commercial endeavors. Do not go any great distance without first checking whether things have changed since this book was written. Likewise, don't assume that a store is located in an outlet center because a similar center has that store as an anchor establishment. Leasing arrangements vary from state to state and from center to center.

If stores are in an area affected by tourism—as are many near amusement parks and other attractions—their hours fluctuate with the tourist season. Be prepared for reduced hours in the off-season. Many stores accept credit cards; when they do not, the listing will so indicate. Take along cash or your checkbook with at least two forms of proper identification, usually a driver's license and a major credit card. Be aware that some stores do not accept personal checks; look for that information in the listing. Most outlets are fully or partially accessible to shoppers with disabilities. An accessibility heading for each outlet or mall indicates the general conditions readers will encounter.

Outlet shopping is a challenge. In meeting that challenge you and your budget become the winners. This guide provides you with the winning edge in this ongoing money-saving adventure. Go out, have fun, and save!

State Tourism Information

Illinois Office of Tourism
State of Illinois Center
100 W. Randolf, Suite 3–400
Chicago, IL 60601
(800) 223–0121

Indiana Tourism Division
One North Capitol, Suite 700
Indianapolis, IN 46204
(800) 289–6646

Iowa Division of Tourism
200 E. Grand Avenue
Des Moines, IA 50309
(800) 345–IOWA

Michigan Travel Bureau
P.O. Box 30226
Lansing, MI 48909
(800) 543–2937

Minnesota Office of Tourism
375 Jackson Walkway,
  250 Skyway Level
St. Paul, MN 55101
(800) 657–3700

Missouri Division of Tourism
P.O. Box 1055
Jefferson City, MO 65102
(800) 877–1234

Ohio Division of Travel
  and Tourism
P.O. Box 1001
Columbus, OH 43216–0101
(800) BUCKEYE

Wisconsin Division of Tourism
123 W. Washington Avenue
P.O. Box 7970
Madison, WI 53707
(800) 432–TRIP

Finding New Manufacturers

Many manufacturers are subsidiaries or divisions of large corporations. We include a list of corporate affiliations to enable you to shop with greater knowledge and understanding of the brand names you're likely to find in factory stores.

Knowing corporate affiliations will enable you to anticipate the brand names you can expect to find in a direct factory outlet. For example, suppose you're planning a trip to one of the Oxford Industries outlets. In checking your list, you learn that besides Oxford Collection goods, you should also find Lanier Clothes, B. J. Design Concepts, Polo for Boys, and Holbrook Shirts. Thus, you are able to prepare a comprehensive shopping list before taking a buying trip.

Being acquainted with connections among apparel manufacturers will also help you recognize the quality and value of labels that may be unfamiliar. For instance, you may buy Evan Picone apparel because you feel it is well made, but have you ever tried Palm Beach clothing, which is part of the same corporation? When shopping and finding these new labels, you can now take a fresh look at them.

Similarly, if you have outgrown the size range of a favorite manufacturer's apparel, knowing the names of other manufacturers in the same corporation can help you find new clothing with the same quality and value.

This partial list includes some subsidiaries and divisions of corporations that we thought would be of interest to you.

U.S. Shoe Corporation
Capezio
Cobbies
Joyce
Amalfi
Pappagallo
Red Cross
Bandolino

Waterford Wedgwood USA
Aynesley
Johnston Brothers
Waterford
Wedgwood

Salant Corporation
Manhattan

Anne Klein
John Henry for Women
John Henry
Perry Ellis
Peters & Ashley

Crystal Brands
Evan Picone
Gant
Haspel/Gant
Palm Beach
Izod LaCoste
Eagle Shirtmakers
Monet
Trifari

Leslie Fay Corporation
Leslie Fay

Breckenridge
Kasper for A.S.L.
Head Sports
Castleberry Knits
Knitivo

VF Corporation
Lee
Vanity Fair
Bassett Walker
Girbaud
Jantzen
Wrangler
Modern Globe

Warnaco
Jack Nicklaus
Chaps by Ralph Lauren
Thane
Hathaway
Puritan Sportswear
Christian Dior
White Stag
Warner
Ungaro

No outlet owner may purchase inclusion in this book. Store inclusion is purely a personal decision on the part of the authors. In addition, some outlets chose not to participate in the compilation of this book, and providing pertinent information was on a purely voluntary basis. Consequently, the extent of information may vary from profile to profile and outlet to outlet.

Authors' visits to stores are unannounced and anonymous so as to avoid special treatment or promotional influence. Future editions of this guide will allow for additions of new factory stores. To have a store considered for inclusion, please address questions or comments to The Globe Pequot Press, P.O. Box 833, Old Saybrook, Connecticut 06475. All inquiries will be given careful consideration for future editions. References from readers will be greatly appreciated.

Profiles

Aca Joe
Unisex clothing featuring Marithe and Francois Gerbaud and Coogi sweaters.

Accessories Outlet
Earrings, headbands, sunglasses, purses, T-shirts, sterling silver, and more, all at reduced prices.

Action Homewares Outlet
Discounted housewares and cookware.

Adams Factory Shoe Outlet
The finest quality men's and women's footwear. Slight blemish defects and overruns of current styles are purchased from the best manufacturers and sold at savings up to 75 percent off retail. In business over forty-five years; extra-wide, extra-large, and unusual sizes are a specialty.

Adolfo II
Designer wear for the well-dressed woman, direct from the manufacturer at 20 to 50 percent off. Noted labels include Adolfo II, Rafael, Donna Karan, and Dressy Tessy.

Adrienne Vittadini
Top-quality, ready-to-wear women's apparel and accessories at least 40 percent off department store prices.

Aileen
Manufacturer-owned and -operated outlet for women's sportswear in missy, petite, and women's sizes. American-made, first-quality goods are discounted 35 to 70 percent off suggested retail prices.

Air Step/Buster Brown
Specializing in Air Step and Buster Brown shoes for men, women, and children.

Ambassador Crystal

Crystal and gold items offered at a discount.

Ambrosia Chocolate & Cocoa

Fine chocolates, cocoa, and confections. Fresh homemade fudge, candies, baking, and candy making supplies, plus handmade gifts.

American Tourister/Buxton

Top-quality luggage and travel products are discounted from 40 to 70 percent. Items include "gorilla tough" hard-sided luggage, soft-sided luggage, attachés and sports bags in a variety of sizes. Ships anywhere in the United States.

AMPI Morning Glory Farms

Top-grade Wisconsin colby, monterey jack, and flavored longhorn cheeses are available at this manufacturer's outlet, including their trademark Co-Jack longhorn. Discounts are based on size and quantity, but prices are considerably less than retail.

Amy Stoudt

Personal service and first-quality fashions for the large size woman in sizes 14W–32W. Current-season clothing for work, evening, or weekends discounted 20 to 50 percent off comparable everyday prices.

Andercraft Woods

Direct from the factory, first-quality, nationally sold Wisconsin white cedar planters, mailboxes, birdhouses, feeders, and nativity stables at savings up to 50 percent.

Anderson Fabrics

Makers of top-quality designer household fabrics as well as blinds, shades, and verticals, all at 50 percent off suggested retail. Coordinated wallpaper, dust ruffles, pillow shams, quilted spreads, and curtains are carried. Special order fabrics and custom labor services are 25 percent off retail. Drapery hardware is 15 percent off.

Anko Also

High fashion Anko women's apparel with an extensive accessory collection to coordinate, direct from the manufacturer, from 20 to 50 percent off.

Anne Klein
Manufacturer's savings of up to 50 percent on first-quality Anne Klein II apparel and accessories including jewelry, perfume, watches, and handbags.

Annie's Son Shoes
Name-brand shoes for men, women, and children, plus accessories.

Ann Taylor Clearance Center
Women's fine apparel and shoes featuring the Ann Taylor label, as well as Tahari and Nichole Miller fashions.

The Answer
Famous-maker dresses and casual clothing for large-size women.

Arrow Factory Store
Save 30 to 70 percent off suggested retail on Arrow dress, sport, and knit shirts. Gold Toe socks, sweaters, pants, and ties are also discounted.

Athlete's Foot Outlet
Sporting apparel and shoes with famous brands such as Nike, Umbro, and Asics.

Athletic Shoe Factory
Clothing, accessories, and brand name athletic shoes for the serious and part-time athlete.

Aunt Mary's Yarns
Needlework supplies such as yarns, crewel, and needlepoint, along with craft materials, art supplies, and silk and dried floral supplies at discounted prices.

Aureus Factory Store
First-quality and near-perfect seconds of sportswear by Aureus for men

and by Aurea for women at savings of 30 to 60 percent. Merchandise includes shirts, sweaters, pants, shorts, and golf shoes.

Avirex
An American Classics factory outlet that discounts 20 to 60 percent off suggested retail on leather bomber and flight jackets, jeans, denims, knits, and outdoor clothing.

Bag & Baggage
Luggage and handbag outlet featuring a complete selection of famous-name luggage, business cases, handbags, and small leather goods at 20 to 50 percent off suggested retail.

Bally
Top-of-the-line Bally brand shoes, clothing, leather goods, executive cases, and luggage.

Banister Shoes
Factory-direct prices, with savings up to 50 percent on Capezio, Pappagallo, Mushrooms, Liz Claiborne, Freeman, and nearly forty other manufacturers of men's and women's name-brand casual and athletic footwear.

Barbizon
Fine lingerie direct from the manufacturer at 30 to 60 percent savings. Quality fabrication offers detailing, embroidery, and laces.

Bass Shoes
Savings of 25 percent or more off the retail price on full-grain leather Weejuns, Bucs, Sunjuns sandals, and other classic footwear and accessories. Merchandise has the quality and style that has been a Bass tradition for more than a hundred years.

Bed, Bath & Beyond
Complete line of home furnishings and accessories.

Bemidji Woolen Mills
First- and second-quality men's and women's woolen garments, includ-

ing wool sport shirts and heavy-lined hunting coats, are available at 20 to 50 percent below retail. Some are made in the mill; others are name brands such as Woolrich, Pendleton, and Hudson Bay. Yarns by the pound, sweaters, wool batting, and remnants are also stocked.

Benetton/United Colors of Benetton
Save up to 50 percent on a large selection of summer and winter international clothing fashions, available year-round.

Bergquist Imports, Inc.
The factory-owned outlet features first quality and seconds in Scandinavian design dinnerware, mugs, tiles, and plates. Discounts average 30 percent.

Bermans Leather Outlet
Leather products for men, women, children, and big and tall.

Better Homes and Gardens Outlet
The outlet carries books, magazines, videos, and craft supplies, all at greatly reduced prices. Subjects include home improvement, home decorating, cooking, crafts, gardening, and children's books.

Bigsby and Kruthers
Better menswear, including Giorgio Armani, Hugo Boss, Perry Ellis, and Yves Saint Laurent.

Black & Decker
Small appliances, tools, and hardware at up to 35 percent off everyday prices.

Bon Worth
Name-brand missy and women's sportswear. Discounts can run up to 70 percent. Bon Worth products are from 30 to 60 percent off regular retail.

Bookland
Over 100,000 books. From selected *New York Times* best-sellers to magazines and paperbacks. Everything in the store is discounted up to 80 or 90 percent.

Book Warehouse
National deep-discount chain that sells new books at 50 to 90 percent off publisher's suggested retail prices. Reading material for all tastes, including children's books, cookbooks, and self-improvement selections.

Bootery Outlet
Up to 50 percent savings everyday on men's and women's brand-name fashion footwear. Handbags and accessories are also value priced.

Boot Factory
Code West and Laredo boots, with slight imperfections, for men, women, and children are discounted from 30 to 50 percent. First-quality western wear, leather goods, and accessories are also stocked.

Bostonian Hanover
Men's and women's dress and casual shoes and shoe care items from the manufacturer. Featured name brands include Bostonian, Hanover, Rockport, Deer Stag, Timberland, and Naturalizer discounted from 10 to 60 percent.

Boston Trader Kids
Traditionally inspired, first-quality apparel for children. For girls sizes infant through pre-teen and boys sizes infant through 20 there are tops, pants, shorts, dresses, jumpers, rompers, and swimwear, discounted direct from the manufacturer.

Boston Traders
Factory-direct men's and women's clothing, including outerwear, big and tall apparel, belts, luggage, and accessories.

Bouquet's of Red Wing
Huge savings of 30 to 70 percent off retail prices of wood products and folk art dolls manufactured in Minnesota and sold in fine gift stores located in Minnesota and Wisconsin.

Boyd's Crystal Art Glass
Factory-direct, first-quality collectible antique glass figurines and paperweight reproductions in a wide spectrum of colors. Take a free tour and watch craftsmen at one of America's most respected glass factories.

Brands
Discounted quality apparel and accessories for men and women, all at 30 to 70 percent off retail. Brand names featured are Perry Ellis, Chaps by Ralph Lauren, Nancy Heller, Sanyo, Bill Blass, Michii Moon, Leon Levin, and Lakeland.

Brass Factory Outlet
High-quality, solid brass accessories for home and office, available at factory-direct prices. Nautical accessories, gifts, and decorations to choose from, too.

Brass Town
Brass accents at substantial discounts.

The Brighter Side
Exclusive collection of oil lamps and oils at manufacturer's discounts of up to 70 percent every day. Accessory parts such as wicks, burners, and chimneys are stocked, along with sconces and floral accent rings.

Bristol County
Ladies tailored American-made suits, skirts, slacks, and blazers direct from the manufacturer.

Brooks Fashion Company Store
Casual fashions for women and juniors from Brooks stores.

Brownberry Bakery Outlet
Substantial savings of 30 to 40 percent off retail on bakery overruns. All-natural breads, rolls, croutons, stuffing, and other fine bakery products are brought in fresh daily.

Brown Shoe Outlet
Brown Shoe company outlet offering Naturalizer, LifeStride, Natural Sport, and Connie footwear at savings of 30 to 50 percent every day.

Bruce Alan Bags, Etc.
Indulge in luxury leather handbags from the finest designers at 25 to 45 percent off regular retail. Choose from handbags, accessories, wallets, attachés, travel ware, and hard-to-find notions.

Bubbles and Scents Factory Outlet
Savings up to 60 percent off retail for this manufacturer's line of leading fragrances and luxury bath products with nationally known names such as Clair Burke, Elizabeth Arden, Rigaud Bioessence, Pierre Cardin, and Vita Bath. Goods are overruns, discontinued items, and production seconds. A selection of gift items is also available.

Bugle Boy Outlet
Bugle Boy and Vincente Nesi contemporary sportswear, shoes, and accessories. Factory owned and operated, with 20 to 60 percent savings.

Burlington Coat Factory Warehouse
Famous-maker women's, children's, and men's wear, mostly first quality and current season. Coats, dresses, sportswear, handbags, linens, and bath accessories are discounted 25 to 70 percent. Some stores carry a full line of brand-name shoes. Also London Fog raincoats for men and women at tremendous savings.

Burlington Shoes
Savings of 20 to 60 percent over other retail stores on famous brand shoes for men, women, and children. Choose from dress or casual styles and a large selection of brand-name athletic shoes for men and women.

Burnham Glove Factory Outlet
Direct from the manufacturer, over 1,000 styles of gloves and mittens. First-quality and irregular goods as well as buy-outs of dress, golf, garden, ski, work, and play gloves for men, women, and children. Discounts range from 50 to 75 percent off retail.

Calvin Klein
Men's and women's designer sportswear at mostly 50 percent off. Calvin Klein jeans at 30 to 70 percent savings.

Cambridge Dry Goods
Updated traditional women's sportswear, activewear, and careerwear at 30 to 70 percent savings on Cambridge Dry Goods, Cambridge Sports Club, Cambridge Spirit, and J. J. Farner labels.

Camelot Music Outlet
Complete line of music and accessories, including cassettes and compact discs, music and movie videos, and posters, plus cassette, disc, and video holders.

Cape Isle Knitters
Top-quality, name-brand sweaters and knit goods in 100 percent cotton. Men and women save with direct manufacturer discounts of 30 to 50 percent.

Capers
Men's and women's casual clothing.

Capezio Shoes
Take the pinch out of buying this famous manufacturer's women's shoes. Most stores carry Bandolino, Capezio, Gundie, Pappagallo, Liz Claiborne, Evan Picone, Esprit, and Zodiac shoes.

Captree
Women's missy and junior sportswear and accessories with savings of 25 to 60 percent.

Card and Gift Outlet
American Greeting cards, gift items, and novelties.

Carlson's Christmas Collection
Where Christmas lives all year round. Exquisite hand-made accessories and giftware plus merchandise from Fitz and Floyd, Baldwin, and Virginia Metalcrafters.

Carole Hochman Lingerie
Direct from the manufacturer, everyday savings of 40 to 70 percent on America's leading fashion intimate apparel. Name brands include Christian Dior, Carole Hochman, Sara Beth lingeries, and Lily of France bras.

Carolina Designs Factory Outlet
Lenox candles of every size and description, plus candle holders, flower rings, Carolina soaps, bathroom accessories, and gift items always 30 to 70 percent off. Lenox is the largest candle manufacturer in the country.

Carousel Animal Fair Factory Outlet
It's a real zoo here, with plush, cuddly stuffed animals. The manufacturer sells overstock and discontinued styles at 60 percent off, often more. T-shirts, night shirts, and slippers (even overstuffed animal paw types and cartoon characters) round out the selection of merchandise.

Carroll Reed
Shop the catalog outlet for everyday savings of 30 to 50 percent off updated classic, quality fashions and shoes for the traditional woman.

Carter's Childrenswear
A full line of children's playwear, sleepwear, and underwear, newborn to size 14, and complete layette products. Save 20 to 60 percent direct from the manufacturer.

Casual Male Big and Tall
Affordable brand-name fashions for big and tall men of all ages.

Champion Hanes
Choose from first-quality or slightly imperfect activewear for the whole family, direct from the manufacturer. Colorful sweats, knit tops, T-shirts, socks, and more are 100 percent guaranteed.

Champs Outlet
Sporting apparel, shoes, and athletic equipment, including baseball bats and gloves, golf clubs, and weight benches.

Chaus
Updated, impeccable-quality women's fashions styled with classic lines that aren't outdated next week or next year, all at factory-direct savings.

Chicago Records
Low, low prices and great selection. Over 8,000 cassette tapes, 6,000 compact discs, T-shirts, posters, plus audio and video accessories.

Chico's
Casual cotton clothing for women.

Children's Place
Quality clothing for boys and girls from newborn through size 14. Famous brands such as OshKosh, Health-Tex, and Baby Toys are discounted from 20 to 40 percent.

China Plus
Fine Sango dinnerware from the manufacturer at 20 to 70 percent off retail. Flatwear, drink ware, serving pieces, and gifts from Nikko, International China, Dansk, Nancy Calhoun, F. B. Rogers, and Crisa are also sold at a discount.

Cirage
Women's moderately priced casual and business apparel with the Cirage, Laura and Jayne, and S. K. and Company labels.

Claires Clearance
Ladies' and girls' jewelry and fashion accessories at affordable prices.

Class Perfume
Designer-label fragrances for men and women.

Clothes Outs
In-season, current, first-quality, brand-name sportswear for men and women discounted 20 to 50 percent or more every day.

Clothestime
Junior fashions featuring famous brands such as Bongo Jeans, The Limited, and Italian Club.

Clothing by Farah
Direct from the manufacturer with savings of 50 percent or more off regular retail. Men's suits, sport coats, dress slacks and casualwear. Boys' dress and casual clothing in sizes 4 to 14 and husky sizes.

Coach
Classically styled leather goods and related accessories for men and women direct from the manufacturer, beautifully handcrafted in the best tradition.

Colours by Alexander Julian
Top-line, current style, casual clothing for men, discounted 30 to 70 percent, with the Alexander Julian label.

Columbia Sportswear
Manufacturer-direct seconds, closeouts, and discontinued styles in sportswear, ski wear, and hunting wear at discounts from 30 to 40 percent off regular retail.

The Company Store
Large selection of down-filled coats, jackets, vests, and booties. Company Store label items at a minimum of 50 percent off.

The Cookie Jar Cookie Outlet
Save up to 65 percent on fresh-from-the-factory bulk cookies. Crackers, snacks, candies, and cookie jars are also available.

Corning/Revere
Excellent savings on corning glass products such as Corningware, Pyrex, Corelle, and Visions, plus the broadest assortment of Revere accessories.

Cory Everson Fitness Fashions
Unisex line of body building, fitness, and casualwear fashions.

Cosco Factory Outlet Store
Cosco folding furniture, tray tables, counter and step stools, carts, cribs, play pens, and baby products are available direct from the manufacturer at 30 to 70 percent off suggested retail. Most merchandise is first quality. Some pieces are returned goods, inspected for damage and sold at further discounts.

Cotton Mill Factory Outlet
Towels, sheets, curtains, linens, bedspreads, and much more at savings up to 70 percent. Mostly first-quality goods with some slight irregulars direct from the manufacturer.

Country Club Outlet
Better men's and women's activewear and golf equipment discounted

40 to 50 percent. Merchandise is mostly first-quality with some over-runs and closeouts. Name brands include LaMode, Hogan, Antigua, Izod, Hogan, Wilson, Etonic, and Titleist.

County Seat
Overstock men's and women's styles from County Seat stores.

Crazy Horse
Contemporary sweaters and sportswear in women's sizes 4 to 16. Select group of men's sweaters. Everyday savings of 40 to 60 percent off regular retail.

Create-a-Book
Original, personalized, thirty-six-page children's storybooks. Child's name, age, hometown, friends, and family are worked into the story line. Other personalized products.

Crown Jewels
Quality, selection, and value on fine fashion jewelry. Most items offered at 50 percent off the ticketed price.

Crystal Works
Elegant accents, home decor, and tableware. Significant savings from 20 to 60 percent on Nachtmann's finest-quality, full-lead European crystal.

c.s.o.
Junior fashions—sportswear, dresses, jackets, coats, lingerie, accessories, and more at 20 to 70 percent off retail prices.

CW Company
Comfortable apparel in today's modern styles for today's confident women at savings of 30 to 50 percent.

Dansk
Seconds, overstocks, and limited edition classic Dansk designs in flatware, glassware, cookware, dinnerware, and gifts are discounted up to 60 percent.

Danskin Factory Outlet

Bodywear, tights, sportswear, and hosiery from the manufacturer at savings of 30 to 70 percent off retail.

Dayton's Outlet Store

Dented items, discontinued styles, and returned goods, all culled from Dayton's retail stores, are stocked at their outlet. Look for furniture, electronics, appliances, carpeting, and rugs. Good deals get better during "Warehouse Sales."

Denmark Imports

Quality life-style furniture imported from Denmark. Savings up to 50 percent off retail prices on desks plus bedroom and office furniture, including a complete line of bookcases.

Designer Brands Accessories

Jewelry and accessories.

Diamonds Unlimited

Buy fine jewelry items from the manufacturer at the same wholesale prices retail jewelers pay.

Diane Gilman

Machine washable, 100 percent silk sportswear, dresses, and intimate apparel in missy, petite, and women's sizes.

Dicken's Books

New York Times best-sellers in hardcover and paperback, plus other books, all at tremendous savings.

District Factory Outlet

New furniture and mattresses are purchased by the trailerload from factory floors. Bedroom, living room, and dining room sets, lamps, bunk beds, recliners, and more are among the goods available. The first-quality merchandise is discounted 50 to 80 percent off retail.

Dr. Tavel's One Hour Optical

"One-hour glasses without the one-hour price." Prices generally 20 to

70 percent lower than comparable retail on glasses, contact lenses, and eye exams. Goods all first quality. Special offers like "the $1.00 spare."

Dollar Discount Store
Closeout merchandise at closeout prices, up to 80 percent off. There's a little of everything: housewares, hardware, food, cosmetics, greeting cards, seasonal goods, and more.

Donna Karan
Company store features DKNY designer women's apparel and accessories.

Dress Barn/Dress Barn Woman
Name brand women's fashion labels, always discounted 20 to 50 percent. Labels like Liz Claiborne, Silk and Company, Guess?, Nilani, and many more provide a wide variety of updated fashions. Dress Barn Woman stocks sizes 14 to 24.

Eagle's Eye
Ladies designer fashions from the famous manufacturer at 40 to 60 percent off. Sportswear, activewear, and careerwear in overproduced colors and styles with some irregulars.

Eddie Bauer
Real Eddie Bauer at unreal savings of 40 to 70 percent. Merchandise is first-quality and slightly flawed overstock apparel and gear from national catalog and retail stores.

E.J. Plum
Designer socks deliciously priced.

Ekco Housewares
Baker's Secret and Best Results bakeware seconds are discounted up to 50 percent. Other closeouts and seconds from the Ekco Housewares product line are available at a discount.

Elaine's
Custom floral and interior designs plus gifts and decorative accessories,

mostly hand-made by floral designer/interior decorator Elaine Wolven. Goods are all first quality and are discounted 25 percent.

El-Bee Shoe Outlet

Men's and women's famous brand first-quality and buy-out shoes like Reebok, Nike, L. A. Gear, Hush Puppies, Florsheim, Dingo, Calico, Connie, Joyce, Pappagallo, and many others are discounted every day 15 to 60 percent off department store prices.

Esprit Direct

First-quality jeans, sportswear, activewear, and shoes direct from this top manufacturer for children and teens and women desiring an environmentally correct line of clothing. Expect savings of 30 to 70 percent off all samples and closeouts.

Etienne Aigner

Women's quality fashion footwear, handbags, apparel, and accessories at 30 percent off.

Evan Picone/Palm Beach/Gant

First-quality, name-brand tailored clothing, sportswear, and accessories for men and women, all current season fashions. Labels include Evan Picone, Palm Beach, Gant, and Eagle. Ladies' blazers, skirts, slacks, blouses, sweaters, and Monet/Trifari/Marvella jewelry. Factory direct savings at 30 to 70 percent off suggested retail.

Everitt Knitting Mill Outlet Store

Straight from the factory, Everitt Knitting Company offers first-quality, seconds, and overruns in knit headwear, scarves, gloves, socks, and garments. Discounts average 50 to 75 percent. Knit fabric, trims, yarns, and notions are also available.

Factory Card Outlet

Quality party supplies, gift wrap, greeting cards, and gifts at a discount of 20 percent off the suggested retail, with greeting cards discounted at 50 percent.

Factory Direct Outlet *see* Fostoria Glass Outlet

Factory Linens
True outlet that carries kitchen, table, bed, and bath linens from Ritz and Ritz Royal with 30 to 40 percent discounts.

Factory Shoe Outlet
Discounted shoes for women and children. brand-names include Jumping Jacks, Little Capezios, Nikes, Reeboks, Bernardo, and Moxees.

Famous Brands Housewares
The complete kitchen store featuring more than 4,000 quality household products, including cookware, tableware, and kitchen gadgets, all at fantastic savings.

Famous Footwear
Guarantees the best prices on brand-name shoes for the entire family. Boots and dress, casual, and athletic shoes are stocked. Featured brands include Reebok, Nike, Adidas, Jacqueline, Mushrooms, Candies, Nunn Bush, and more at everyday savings of 10 to 50 percent.

Famous Name Gifts
Something for every age group from stickers and buttons to fireplace tools and German imports. Popular gift items are at 25 to 50 percent savings with solid brass items, porcelain dolls, and Christmas ornaments at 50 percent off marked retail.

F & M Distributors
Noticeably cheaper than discount stores on first-quality health and beauty aids, cosmetics, pet supplies, film processing, greeting cards, and so much more. Savings average around 35 to 70 percent. Double coupons and 10 percent senior savings are offered.

Fanny Farmer
Almost perfect Fanny Farmer chocolates, fudge, nuts, bulk chocolates, holiday, and nonchocolate candy at 25 to 50 percent off suggested retail.

Farah Factory Store
Farah men's and boys' apparel. Boys' sizes 4 to 12, prep, husky, and young men's sizes. Farah brands include Farah, W.F., Savanne, E'Joven

and N.P.W. direct from the manufacturer with discounts from 35 to 40 percent.

Farberware

Manufacturer's direct prices on Farberware cookware, well below suggested retail.

Faribo Woolens

A wide selection of first-quality, irregular, and discounted mill blankets and throws. Famous-maker men's, women's, and children's clothing runs 15 to 25 percent below department store prices.

Fashion Factory Outlet

Women's current style, designer-label apparel at 20 to 70 percent off suggested retail. Office, dress, and casualwear are stocked.

Fashion Flair

Izod/LaCoste, Ship 'N Shore, and Monet apparel and accessories for the family, with savings of 30 to 60 percent off suggested retail.

Fieldcrest Cannon

Towels, kitchen linens, comforters, blankets, sheets, and more are available in a spectrum of colors. First quality, closeouts, and imperfects, all at factory-direct savings of 40 to 60 percent. Pillows, mattress pads, shower curtains, and accessories for bed and bath are excellent values.

Fila

Active Italian sportswear for men and women consisting of samples, defectives, overruns, and past season merchandise at 40 to 50 percent off.

Filene's Basement

Designer labels at discount prices. Look for current fashions discounted at 20 to 60 percent off for men, women, and juniors. Petite and plus-size clothing available, as well as accessories and shoes.

The Finish Line

Men's, women's, and children's athletic shoes and apparel at outstanding prices. College logo apparel and accessories, plus socks and shoe care products.

Fitz and Floyd

This manufacturer's fine housewares, tableware, teapots, and other merchandise are available at savings from 30 to 50 percent off retail.

Flambeau Outlet Store

The Flambeau factory produces, and their outlet sells, plastic tackle boxes, fishing boxes and buckets, waterfowl and hunting decoys, Artbin storage containers, packaging and storage systems, ProTech golf bags, and Duncan YoYos and toys. Goods range from first-quality to irregulars, buy outs, and seconds.

Florence Eiseman

An outlet for children's wear emphasizing simplicity, quality, and comfort as only interpreted by this designer.

Florsheim

Choose from a large selection of dress, casual, and athletic shoes in sizes 6 to 15 and A to EEE widths. Direct-from-the-factory savings on first quality, closeouts, and irregulars are 50 to 75 percent.

Footsaver Shoe Outlet

Ladies' Footsaver and Barefoot Freedom shoes in a huge selection of styles and sizes. All shoes made in the U.S.A., mostly first quality with some irregulars. Outlet specializes in ladies' all-leather orthopedic shoes.

Fostoria Factory Outlet

An assortment of first-quality and seconds stemware, giftware, tableware, crystal, and dinnerware direct from the manufacturer with savings from 50 to 70 percent.

14 Plus Pizazz

Though not a factory outlet, this store has Bonnie & Bill, Chez, French Vanilla, and Barry Ashley brand-name women's fashions, size 14 plus, discounted 20 to 50 percent every day. Mostly first-quality goods with some irregulars and seconds.

Fox River Glove Outlet Store

Leather gloves and mittens from the factory with discounts up to 50 percent. Irregulars and overruns of Wigwam socks, Chic jeans, Spaulding jackets, dress gloves, and first-quality Minnetonka moccasins are sold at discount prices.

Fragrance Cove
Upscale, department store fragrances at discounts up to 60 percent.

Fragrance World
World-famous men's and women's fragrances, cosmetics, and accessories, all at discounts of 20 to 60 percent off suggested retail.

Frugal Frank's
Brand-name shoes for the entire family with discounts of 20 to 40 percent off regular retail prices.

Fuller Brush
Save 20 to 50 percent every day on famous Fuller Brush mops, brooms, brushes, chemicals, and personal care products. Over eighty-two years' experience in supplying households with quality products allows Fuller Brush to extend a 100 percent satisfaction guarantee.

Full Size Fashions
Affordability and fashion go hand in hand to give the stylish edge to the full-figured woman. First-quality merchandise is discounted 20 to 50 percent.

Fureal Leathers
The Midwest's largest selection of men's and women's leathers, furs, and motorcycle garments at everyday savings of 50 to 70 percent. Big men's sizes to 60. Satisfaction guaranteed.

Gabel's Discount Men's Wear
Jaymar-Ruby men's merchandise, Sansabelt slacks, sport coats, shirts, and sweaters are discounted 30 to 50 percent. Goods are all first quality.

Galt Sand
Choose from a large selection of upscale activewear for men and women at savings up to 70 percent off suggested retail.

Gant Company Store
Updated men's sportswear, featuring dress shirts, sport shirts, knits, rugbys, sweaters, and slacks.

Garage Outlet
Men's casual clothing from Boss, Jordache, and Levi's.

GeGe's
Discounted apparel for women.

Generra
Upscale men's, women's, and children's apparel, men's footwear, young men's ties and belts, and hosiery for men and women.

Gentlemen's Wear House
Manufacturer of men's American-made suits, sport coats, and slacks at 30 to 50 percent off.

Geoffrey Beene
Dress, casual, and relaxed life-style fashions for men from one of America's leading designers, with savings of up to 50 percent off comparable retail.

Gift Outlet
First-quality giftware and home decorating accessories featuring brass, crystal, porcelain, and more, all at 30 to 70 percent below retail.

Gilligan O'Malley
High-quality ladies' sleepwear, lounge wear, and robes in alluring styles and colors direct from the manufacturer at 40 to 60 percent off.

Gitano
Savings up to 50 percent, direct from the manufacturer, on casual and active sportswear for the whole family. Gloria Vanderbilt and E. J. Gitano are among the labels stocked in sizes for men, kids, juniors, and misses, as well as maternity and plus sizes. Underwear, outerwear, socks, bodywear, and other accessories are available.

Graham Industries Home Furnishings

Factory-direct lamps and shades, furniture, wallpaper, bedding and framed pictures are among the variety of goods offered. First-quality goods are discounted 25 percent. Seconds and irregulars are marked and sold at greater discounts. Lamp repair and lampshade re-covering services are available.

Great Midwest Craftmarket

Affordable, handcrafted, first-quality gifts and accessories created in clay, metal, wood, fiber, paper, glass, and leather. Many one-of-a-kind pieces. Special year-round "Christmas Corner."

Great Outdoor Clothing

Quality, name-brand outdoor apparel for the entire family at 30 to 60 percent off.

Grey Goose

Country collectibles gift store.

Group USA

Top-label dress and business clothing for women.

Guess?

Casual fashions for men, women, juniors, and children.

Haas-Jordan Company

America's oldest umbrella manufacturer offers discounts of 40 to 50 percent on first-quality patio, folding, golf, photo, and personal umbrella overruns in their only company-owned store. Seconds receive discounts of up to 70 percent.

Haeger Potteries Outlet

Factory-owned and -operated store with high-quality ceramics such as lamps, vases, and decorating accessories. Most goods are seconds, discontinued, or one-of-a-kind test samples.

Handbag Company Outlet

Handbags, hosiery, and accessories from Liz Claiborne, Espirt, Stone Mountain, Brio, and Barganza.

Handbag Factory Outlet
A factory-direct source for handbags and a wide assortment of earrings, necklaces, bracelets, sunglasses, and many other accessories at 20 to 50 percent off retail prices.

Hanes Activewear *see* Champion Hanes

harvé benard
A wide selection of women's and men's designer apparel, accessories, and furnishings, all at up to 60 percent off suggested retail. Stylish seasonal selections in most sizes.

Hathaway
Geoffrey Beene, Jack Nicklaus, Warners, Christian Dior, Olga, Thane, White Stag, Speedo, Chaps, Puritan, Hathaway, and Pringle are brandnames of the first-quality merchandise produced by this leading manufacturer's many divisions. Expect discounts of 30 to 60 percent off original prices.

Head Factory Outlet
Save 35 percent on ski, tennis, running, and golf fashions for men and women from America's leading sports manufacturer.

Helly-Hansen
Manufacturers of apparel, activewear, and accessories for cross-country and downhill skiing, biking, sailing, running, and other activities at 30 to 60 percent off.

Hensen Lingerie Factory Store
Quality Hensen Kickernick lingerie at 45 to 75 percent savings direct from the manufacturer. Items include sleepwear, daywear, foundations, panties, and bras.

He-Ro Group
Designer-label casual and business clothing, specializing in party and fancy dresses.

Herrschners Factory Outlet
Premiere supplier of needlework, craft kits, and accessories offers goods

to the public through their outlet store and factory. Outlet discounts are up to 50 percent.

Hickey-Freeman
Men's apparel direct from the manufacturer, discounted 30 to 70 percent.

Hit or Miss
First-quality, current season women's blazers, skirts, slacks, dresses, suits, and coordinating separates from brand-name manufacturers at 20 to 50 percent below department store prices.

Home Decor Outlet
Curtains, draperies, blankets, pillows, towels, sheets, and bathroom and kitchen accessories, all at discount prices.

Houseware Outlet
A large assortment of Chef Craft gadgets, bake ware, and tumblers. Selections from Anchor, Ekco, Colonial Kitchen, Wixon spices, and Sterilite, various microwave accessories, glassware, and candles. Stemware at 20 to 70 percent off.

Hush Puppies Factory Direct
Name-brand dress, casual, and athletic footwear for the entire family with 20 to 50 percent savings off suggested retail prices.

I. B. Diffusion
Women's apparel and accessories at 30 to 70 percent off. Manufacturer's labels include I. B. Diffusion, I. B. Diffusion Sports, Santoria, Marc Allen, Joye & Fun, and Rediffusion.

Indiana Glass Outlet
First-quality, irregular, and overstock Indiana Glass and Colonial Glass comes straight from the factory. Prices start at 19 cents. Glasses, pitchers, ashtrays, candlesticks, dishes, candles, and other household glassware is discounted 50 percent.

Izod
Factory direct to you, Izod/LaCoste fashions for men, women, and children at savings of 30 to 60 percent off manufacturer's suggested retail.

J & S Liquidators

Solid oak reproduction cabinetry. Can be first-quality, irregulars, or closeouts.

Jaymar

Jaymar, Sansabelt, Racquet Club, and Lady Sansabelt fashions direct from the manufacturer at 30 to 70 percent savings.

J. C. Penney Outlet Store

Penney catalog merchandise, overstocked or discontinued, is available at substantial savings. Look for men's, women's, and children's shoes and apparel, sporting goods, furniture, and domestic goods. New merchandise comes in daily. The selection is always different. Returned catalog merchandise, due to wrong color, size, or style, is also carried at the outlet. A few items with corrected mechanical or electrical defects, missing parts, or damages from shipment are also stocked. Check for specific warranty details at each outlet store.

J. Crew

Super savings of 30 to 70 percent on classic apparel and sportswear for men and women direct from the manufacturer.

Jefferson Industries, Inc.

Discounts of 50 percent or more on brand-name carpet mats, room-size remnants, runners, accent rugs and indoor/outdoor carpet direct from the manufacturer. Merchandise is irregular or seconds.

Jennings Decoy Company

Large selection of first-quality, direct-from-the-factory decorative wildlife gifts, decoys, and carving supplies. Customized orders are accepted.

Jersild Factory Store

Knit goods for the entire family, direct from the factory at discounts of up to 70 percent off retail. Merchandise includes first-quality goods as well as irregulars, closeouts, overruns, and one-of-a-kind samples. Wool throws, hats, mittens, scarves, and socks are also featured.

The Jewel Case
Monet jewelry, belts, and bohemian glass at savings from 40 to 50 percent off retail.

Jewelies
Huge assortment of costume jewelry for women discounted at 40 to 70 percent below regular retail. Similar savings are available on gift items, cards, watches, perfumes, clocks, key chains, scarves, and more.

JH Collectibles
For the fashion-conscious woman. Better sportswear and separates in sizes 2 to 16 and a full line of petites at 30 to 60 percent off suggested retail.

Jim & Chuck's Boot Outlet
Name-brand leather boots, jackets, belts, and hats at everyday discounts from 30 to 60 percent off regular retail.

Joan & David
Shoes, boots, belts, bags, and clothing for women. Also David & Joan products for men.

Jockey
Jockey label underwear and sportswear for men, women, and children.

John Henry & Friends
Designer fashions for men and women including John Henry, Perry Ellis, Thomson, Nino Cerruti, Liberty of London, Peters and Ashley, and Pierre Cardin.

Johnston & Murphy
Better men's shoes and accessories from the manufacturer.

Jonathan Logan
Misses- and petite-size famous-label careerwear, dresses, activewear, suits, and outerwear. Famous brands, at savings of 30 to 70 percent, include Villager, R & K Kollection, Misty Harbor, Action Scene, and Rosemarie Reid. Jewelry by Lisner and Encore.

Jones New York
Save 30 to 70 percent on top-quality women's suits and separates including Jones New York, Dior, Seville, and Jones Wear.

Jordache
This store has the look! Discounts of 30 to 60 percent on casualwear for the entire family.

Jordache Kids
Direct from the manufacturer, kids' wear in infants', toddlers', boys', and girls' sizes.

Joseph & Feiss Company Outlet Store
Men's suits, sport coats, slacks, shirts, ties, tuxedos, and sweaters direct from the manufacturer. Sizes range from 36 to 56 in short, short portly, regular, long, and extra long for first-quality goods discounted 45 to 60 percent off standard retail.

Judy Bond
Sportswear in petite, misses, and Ms. Bond plus sizes at savings of 30 to 70 percent.

Julie's Jewelry
Value-priced, unique costume jewelry and accessories.

Just About Perfect
Men's sportswear and accessories at a discount.

Just Kids Outlet Store
Direct from the factory, with savings of 20 to 60 percent. Quality children's name brands include Her Majesty, Cole for Kids, Camp Beverly Hills, and more.

Just My Size Factory Outlet
Discounted name-brand Just My Size hosiery and lingerie, in sizes 38 to 52 and 1x to 5x, for the full-figured woman.

Just Pants
Hefty discounts of up to 50 percent on first-quality, irregular, and sec-

onds clothes for the whole family. Brand-names include Gap, Lee, Guess?, Bugle Boy, The Limited, and Structure in a broad selection of models and sizes.

Just Sunglasses/Sunshade Optique
Full line of designer sunglasses, including name brands such as Ray Ban and Vuarnet.

Kelli's
Jewelry and giftware from top manufacturers such as Seiko, Nao, Hummel, Fenton, Silver Deer, Cross, Pulsar, and many more, with deep discounts ranging from 20 to 70 percent.

Kenneth Cole Shoes
First-quality men's and women's fashion footwear direct from the manufacturer with savings up to 50 percent. Tremendous savings on handbags and accessories.

Kid Port (Kid Spot)
The number one brand of children's apparel, Health-Tex, comes direct from the manufacturer. Discounts run from 25 to 60 percent off suggested retail on sizes from infant to 14.

Kids Ca'pers
Discounted childrenswear: girls from newborn to size 14, boys from newborn to size 7.

Kids Express
Discounted childrenswear and accessories.

Kids Mart
Deep discounts of 20 to 50 percent on first-quality children's clothing and accessories by famous manufacturers such as OshKosh, Carters, Levi's, Lee, Buster Brown, and more. Gift certificates and gift boxes available.

Kitchen Collection
The widest selection of Wear-Ever cookware and Proctor-Silex appli-

ances. This manufacturer's exclusive outlet offers discounts of 20 to 70 percent on first-quality, select manufacturer's seconds and closeout items.

Kitchen Place
More than 5,000 kitchen gadgets, houseware items, and gifts. Discounted are products from Ekco, Rubbermaid, Corning, Pyrex, and Longchamp crystal, to name a few.

Knits by K.T.
Current ladies' sweaters and knits by Kenneth Too plus sportswear by other famous makers are featured at this factory-owned and -operated store. Misses and large sizes are discounted 25 to 60 percent off regular retail.

Knot Shop
Ties, mostly made of silk, from Bigsby & Kruthers, Geoffrey Beene, Hugo Boss, and more.

Kristina K. Outlet
Designer collection features contemporary styles in natural fabrics for today's sophisticated woman.

LaCrosse Footwear, Inc.
Farm, work, industrial, and protective vinyl and rubber footwear and accessories. Rain and winter boots for the entire family from a Wisconsin manufacturer in business since 1897. Sporting, lightweight, and cold-weather pacs, waders, and hip boots are also offered. LaCrosse products are closeouts, seconds, or irregulars with discounts of up to 40 percent off regular retail.

Lady Slipper Designs Outlet—The Gift Outlet
The wholesalers for nonprofit cottage industry products sold to trend setters like Bloomingdales and Neiman Marcus. Discontinued items and slightly flawed seconds in whimsical soft sculpture (including exquisite black velvet felines) and an Indian birchbark craft line are among items offered at substantial savings.

Lands' End Outlet/Combo/Not Quite Perfect stores

First-quality, overstock, and end-of-season classic sportswear, dress shirts, dresses, childrenswear, and domestic ware with a minimum savings of 20 percent off catalog prices. Not Quite Perfect stores carry items not considered first quality. Initially marked down 40 percent, items are regularly marked down to an additional 75 percent off the first 40 percent. Combo stores carry first-quality, overstock, and discontinued items marked with blue tags; customer returns are marked with green tags.

Langtry

First-quality women's career and casual apparel with brand-names such as Langtry, Christy Girl, and Langtry II.

Lazarus Final Clearance

End-of-season, first-quality clothing for men, women, and children from area Lazarus stores is marked down on a regular basis. Some stores carry electronics and housewares. Discounts start at 25 percent and go to 75 percent off the last ticketed price. Goods change daily.

Leather Factory

The full leather store. Western boots, leather jackets, vests, purses, belts, and many more leather items are discounted 25 to 75 percent every day.

Leather Loft

Luxury leather for less. Savings on handbags, luggage, briefcases, jackets, and designer accessories.

Leather Manor

Choose from a varied array of wallets, handbags, luggage, travel essentials, and briefcases. Save 15 to 70 percent on quality brands like Ashley-Moore, Carryland, Park Avenue, T. Capeli, and others. An exceptional selection of eel skin accessories and leather luggage is available.

Le Creuset

Le Creuset housewares and kitchenware at 40 percent off retail.

Lee Middleton Original Doll Factory Outlet
Seconds of the finest award-winning, original porcelain and vinyl dolls direct from the factory with savings of 75 percent. Local crafts, gifts, and decorating items are also stocked.

L'eggs/Hanes/Bali
Save 20 to 50 percent or more off suggested retail on slightly imperfects, closeouts, and overstocks. Choose from famous brand hosiery, lingerie, socks, underwear, activewear, and more.

Lehmann's Danish Bakery and Kringle Outlet
Award-winning Danish kringle, as featured by Neiman Marcus. Cream puffs, eclairs, Napoleons, tortes, whipped-cream pies, and donuts complete the taste-tempting selection.

Lenox
China, crystal, collectibles, and table top merchandise from the manufacturer. Some first-quality goods; the majority are seconds.

Leslie Fay
Direct from the manufacturer, famous label designer dresses, suits, sportswear, and activewear in misses, petite, and large sizes.

Libbey Glass Factory Outlet
Direct from the factory, Libbey glass tumblers, stemware and glass accessory pieces, with more than 1,500 items in stock. Also L. E. Smith wares, dinnerware, scented candles, and kitchen accessories.

Linen Mill
Discounted table and kitchen linens, decorative pillows, throws, and casual rugs for the home from this quality manufacturer.

Linens 'n Things
A specialty linen store that features quality, name-brand merchandise from leading designers and manufacturers at 20 to 40 percent off regular retail.

Lingerie Factory
Day and evening wear lingerie including name brands such as Olga, Dior, Warner, Elan, Jilandre, Lily of France, and Youth Craft.

Little Red Shoe House

Owned and operated by Wolverine World Wide. Fashionable name-brand footwear for the whole family is discounted 20 to 50 percent off retail. Lines include Hush Puppies, Wolverine Boots, Town & Country women's shoes, Harbor Town, Brooks, Bates, Wimzees, and Rogue River. Frequent special values on the shoes America loves best.

Littman Brothers

Halogen lamps, track lighting, outdoor lights, ceiling fans, and floor lamps, for home or office.

Liz Claiborne

Discounted, first-quality, wear-now styles in misses' and petites' dresses. Substantial savings of up to 75 percent on women's sportswear, handbags, and accessories, plus men's furnishings and sportswear.

London Fog

Owned and operated by the makers of the finest quality rain outerwear, jackets, and coats for men and women. Look for 50 percent off regular retail prices. Men's and women's umbrellas, hats, scarves, sweaters, and other articles are offered at substantial savings.

Loomcraft Home Decorating Fabrics

The Midwest's largest selection of home decorating fabrics. Thousands of bolts in stock. Kirsch drapery hardware, upholstery, drapery supplies, and foam are also discounted.

Macy's Close-Out

Clothing and shoes from Macy's, I. Magnin, and Bullocks stores that have been marked down at least 50 percent.

Madeleine Fashions

Exclusive European fashions for women, in sizes 6 to 18, at reduced prices.

Magnavox

Televisions, stereo equipment, computers, and other consumer electronic equipment manufactured by Magnavox.

Maidenform

Save up to 60 percent on Maidenform first-quality discontinued and closeout bras, panties, camisoles, half slips, sleepwear, daywear, garter belts, and lingerie.

Manhattan Factory Store

First-quality, name-brand apparel for men and women with factory-direct savings of up to 60 percent off retail. Women's brands include Anne Klein, Manhattan, and Lady Arrow, some in plus and petite sizes. Featured men's brands include Manhattan, Perry Ellis, and John Henry.

Mark Cross

Outlet for this top manufacturer's collection of fine handbags, small leather goods, luggage, briefcases, attachés, and more for men and women.

Marshalls

Deep discounter of overruns, irregulars, and discontinued fashions and accessories for the home and the entire family.

Maternity Wearhouse

First-quality complete line for the mother-to-be, discounted 15 to 50 percent below manufacturers suggested retail. Expect to find casual, career, active, and after-five outfits, including lingerie.

Mattress Factory, Inc.

The full line of mattress and futon products is available to the public direct from the factory at 10 percent over wholesale.

Merry Go Round Outlet

Casual clothing for men, women, and juniors, direct from Merry Go Round stores.

Meystel Warehouse

First quality, irregulars, and buy-outs of branded designer apparel for men, women, and children with discounts of 30 to 60 percent. In business since 1925, the store attracts customers by word of mouth, as it does not advertise.

Mid America Shoe Factory Outlet
Brand-name athletic, dress, and casual shoes for the entire family. Top-of-the-line work boots.

Midwest Glass & China Outlet
Savings of up to 50 percent on glassware, china, and silverware from Anchor Hocking, Roseville Pottery, Fiesta, and Homer Laughlin.

Midwestern Sport Togs Outlet
Deerskin gloves, garments, handbags, footwear, and accessories are available at the factory-owned and -operated outlet. Firsts, seconds, and closeouts are discounted from 30 to 50 percent.

Mikasa Factory Store
The factory-direct outlet features a vast selection of dinnerware, crystal, giftware, housewares, and more. Save up to 80 percent.

Milbern Clothing Company
First-quality, in-season tailored clothing for the male or female professional. Suits, sport coats, pants, and more from manufacturers like Palm Beach, Oleg Cassini and Christian Brooks, plus private-label merchandise, sold at 20 to 50 percent off retail. Alterations available at cost.

Mill City Outlet
Lee jeans for the entire family in basic and fashionable styles. Lord Isaacs slacks. Current junior and updated missy looks in tops and outerwear.

Misty Harbor
The factory-owned and -operated outlet has ladies' Misty Harbor outerwear, plus Robbie dresses and sportswear, in first quality and seconds, available year-round, with discounts of 30 to 80 percent.

Mitchell Leather Factory Store
Save up to 60 percent on the latest Samsonite, Skyway, and other quality brand luggage as well as their own manufactured-in-Milwaukee designer briefcases, handbags, and attachés, without the designer label.

Mondi
Fine, European-style women's casual clothing with the Mondi label.

Monterey Mills Outlet
The country's largest selection of deep-pile fur fabrics in first quality, closeouts, overruns, discontinued styles, and substandard items, direct from the mill. Savings are usually 50 percent. Remnants and scrap pieces are available by the pound. Goods available through the mail. A sample of each style and color in the product line is $4.00.

Montgomery Ward Clearance Outlet
Discontinued, reconditioned, and scratched or dented Montgomery Ward major appliances, furniture, electronics, and lawn and garden equipment is substantially discounted.

Multiples
Save 40 to 60 percent off department store prices on Multiples modular "mix and match" knit apparel. First-quality, easy-care, no-iron, one-size-fits-all knits in women's, plus, and children's sizes.

Napier Jewelry
Men's and women's jewelry, fashions, and accessories direct from the manufacturer.

Native Wood Products
Direct from the factory, a selection of seconds and overstocks of oak and walnut kitchen, bath, and home accessories. Prices are a fraction over wholesale.

Natural Footgear
Men's and women's shoes and accessories.

Naturalizer
Timeless, comfortable, lasting-quality footwear that women trust.

Nautica
Factory-direct men's and women's sportswear, activewear, and outerwear at savings of 30 percent off retail.

NCS Shoe Outlet

The latest women's shoes from Nickels, Jazz, Via Spiga, Paloma, Studio Paolo, and Glacee at 50 to 75 percent off.

Nettle Creek Factory Outlet

First-quality, current season bedspreads, decorator pillows, fabric by the yard, and custom-made window dressings are 35 percent off retail. First-quality items can be discounted up to 60 percent. A special clearance section offers discounts up to 70 percent for irregular merchandise. Accessories such as dust ruffles, pillow shams, upholstered headboards, and boudoir furniture are available or can be custom ordered.

Newgate Shirts

A mix of first-quality and irregular dress and sport shirts and blouses are discounted 30 to 50 percent.

Newport Sportswear

Current season, first-quality men's coordinated sportswear, shirts, sweaters, outerwear, and activewear is discounted 35 percent.

New Visions

Sunglasses, reading glasses, sports glasses, and all-weather glasses, all at a discount. Featured accessories include cords, cases, and clip-on glasses.

Nickels Company Store

Mostly first-quality women's shoes and accessories are featured, with discounts up to 50 percent off retail.

Nike

A superb selection of athletic footwear, apparel, and accessories from the manufacturer with discounts from 30 to 50 percent.

9 West

High-quality, value-oriented women's fashion footwear and related items.

Ninth Street Bridal and Formal Outlet

Name-brand gowns for brides, attendants, mothers of the bride, proms, pageants, and social occasions. Savings are up to 70 percent on buy-outs, samples, and liquidations. Everything is off the rack; no orders. Lingerie, invitations, and accessories are also available.

No Name Outlet
Casual clothing for women and juniors.

No Nonsense & More
Family hosiery and sportswear.

North Face
Fine outdoor apparel and equipment. Great prices on rugged sports-wear, outerwear, and ski wear.

Nu-Look Fashions Outlet Store
Men's suits, topcoats, and sport coats at substantial discounts in sizes 36 to 54. All items on the rack are first-quality. Direct from the manu-facturer that supplies J. C. Penney and Federated department stores.

Oak Leather
Leather outerwear for men and women, specializing in lambskin and shearling coats and accessories.

Oilily
Unique clothing and accessories for women and children.

Old Mill Ladies Sportswear
Updated ladies sportswear in coordinates and contemporary separates, dresses, and suits. Sizes range from 4 to 18 and petite sizes 4 to 16. The exclusive factory outlet carries Country Suburbans, Handmacher, Sub-urban Petites, and Weathervane Petites with savings from 25 to 70 per-cent.

Old Time Pottery
An ever-changing variety of wicker baskets, silk flowers and arrange-ments, crafts, lamps, pictures, and pottery. Famous brand-name din-nerware, crystal, cookware, bakeware, and more, all at tremendous savings.

Olga/Warner
Warnaco designer lingerie outlet with first-quality intimate apparel from Olga, Valentino, Warner, and Ungaro at 30 to 70 percent off.

Oneida Factory Store
Super savings ranging from 20 to 70 percent, direct from the manufacturer of stainless and silver-plated flatware, silver-plated holloware, child and baby items, plus a large selection of gifts.

Oops We Goofed
The source for first-quality window coverings. Tremendous savings of 50 to 80 percent off retail on Graber drapery hardware and vertical blinds, Bali micro/mini blinds, custom draperies and valances, custom-quilted bedspreads, and upholstery fabrics.

Oriental Weavers
Manufacturer-direct rugs, handmade in China and Egypt.

OshKosh B'Gosh
Savings of 20 to 50 percent off retail prices on Genuine Article sportswear for the entire family.

Ozcan Sportswear
Men's and women's authentic sportswear.

Paint and Wallpaper Factory Outlet
Nationally advertised name-brand paints at discount prices.

Paper Factory
Party goods, decorations, gift wrap, bows, ribbons, greeting cards, books, games, puzzles, and paper office supplies, all under one roof, with savings up to 50 percent.

Paper Warehouse
Greeting cards, gift wrap, and stationery at discount prices. A complete party center; customized wedding invitations, napkins, plates, and decorations are also stocked.

Pepperidge Farm
Cookies and baked goods from one of America's leading bakers.

Perfumania
Save up to 60 percent on genuine name-brand perfumes, colognes, cosmetics, and skin care products.

Perfume Boutique
Expect a large selection of classic men's and women's fragrance reproductions at 85 percent savings, plus balms, lotions, and atomizers.

Pfaltzgraff Collector's Center
The largest selection of stoneware in America at 10 to 50 percent off. Save on stoneware, glassware, kitchen gadgets, decorative accessories, linens, and housewares. Special prices on Pfaltzgraff collectibles.

Pickard Factory Outlet
The only Pickard China factory outlet, selling only company-manufactured dinnerware and giftware. Blemish-free seconds run from 40 to 60 percent off comparable retail prices. Decorative accessories are made exclusively for the outlet store. Occasionally factory closeouts are stocked.

Pilgrim Silk Flowers
Silk flowers, plants, and trees.

Plumm's
In-season, first-quality styles for misses and juniors are 20 to 50 percent off everyday prices. Stylish, affordable clothes for work, evenings, or weekends.

Plums (Sweaters for Less)
Sweaters, sweaters, sweaters for the entire family. Out-of-season, first-quality, and slightly flawed irregulars consolidated from Winona Knits outlets are featured, with discounts from 30 to 70 percent.

Polly Flinders
Quality hand-smocked girls' dresses in sizes newborn to 14. Matching

hairbows, tights, and panties available to compliment an outfit. Some stores carry boys' sizes 4 months to 4T.

Polo/Ralph Lauren
Fine designer men's, women's, and boys' clothing, home furnishings, leather accessories, and fragrances, with savings of 20 to 50 percent.

Prestige Fragrance & Cosmetics, Inc.
Savings of 25 to 70 percent off suggested retail price on world-famous, brand-name men's and women's fragrances, toiletries, and cosmetics.

Presto Products Factory Outlet
Plastic trash bags, recloseable bags, plastic wrap, cotton swabs, baby wipes, and "private label" first-quality and overrun products discounted 25 to 50 percent below retail.

Publishers Outlet
An assortment of "coffee table" and children's books, mostly hardcover. All are first-quality overruns, with prices 30 to 70 percent below retail.

Purdy Products
An outlet store that offers discounts of 10 to 50 percent on first-quality janitorial products. Brooms and mops; dishwashing, laundry, and hand soaps; pails; and floor care and paper products are among the goods available.

Radio Shack
Discounted electronic equipment, televisions, videocassette players, computers and software, telephones and accessories, and personal stereos.

Rainbow Fashions
Juniors' and misses' sportswear. Merchandise is priced at $13.99 or less, including name brands such as Forenza, Limited Express, Guess?, and many more.

Rawlings
"The Mark Of A Pro." For the sports-minded, NFL-licensed apparel and

equipment plus Rawlings sports equipment and clothing are available at 40 to 60 percent off suggested retail.

Reading Bag Company
Save up to 60 percent every day on luggage and thousands of name-brand handbags, wallets, and business cases.

Reading Shoe Outlet
Save 25 percent or more on full-grain leather Bass footwear, such as Weejuns, Bucs, Sunjuns sandals, as well as other classic footwear and accessories.

Recie's Sample Shop
More than eighty lines of salesmen's samples, with discounts of 30 to 50 percent less than retail. Among the many brands you'll discover are Jones New York, Breckenridge, JH Collectibles, Jantzen, Karen Kane, and many more.

Redwood and Ross Outlet
Service and savings on mostly first-quality goods from Polo, Nautica, Gant, Freedberg, Sero, and Gitman Brothers, with discounts from 30 to 70 percent.

Reebok Factory Outlet Store
The largest selection of athletic and fashion footwear, no matter the sport or activity, plus apparel and accessories for men, women, and children.

Regal Outlet Store/Regal Ware Outlet
Factory-direct housewares, cookware, and kitchen appliances, featuring 30 to 70 percent savings. It's all here: Regal Ware stainless steel, cast aluminum, and drawn aluminum range-top cookware; microwave oven ware and accessories; food processors, electric knives, juicers, coffee makers and corn poppers; vacuum cleaners and air cleaners. Good value on seconds, closeouts, and overruns when available.

Regal Rugs Factory Outlet
Quality workmanship and attractive designs are available direct from

this manufacturer of handcrafted rugs. A complete line of basic and designer rugs, even for large areas, at prices a minimum of 50 to 75 percent off retail. Rugs are irregulars and closeouts because they are a shade off the requisite color criteria, which in no way affects wear.

Remington
Shavers, cutlery, knives, and clocks. Brands include Panasonic, Remington, Braun, Gerber, and Chicago Cutlery.

Ribbon Outlet, Inc.
Over 3,000 varieties of first-quality ribbons and trims in precut lengths or bulk spools or cut by the yard to your dimensions. Distinctive, handcrafted gift items, craft supplies, novelties, and seasonal items are sold by sewing-savvy salespeople at 20 to 70 percent off.

Riverwoods Creations
Factory-direct prices on handcrafted pine furniture including shelves, hutches, deacon's benches, and more.

Rocky Boot Outlet
A true outlet in back of the factory. Save 20 to 50 percent on boots for the whole family.

Rosewood Galleries
First-quality artwork for the home, including custom framing. Discounts on brand names such as Hargrove, Carson, Perez, Cooper, Russell, Cox, and Lee run 25 to 40 percent.

Route 66
Leather clothing, boots, and accessories for men, women, and children.

Royal Doulton
Fine china and crystal from a premiere manufacturer. Mostly first-quality merchandise includes Royal Doulton, Royal Albert, Minton, Bunnykins, Beatrix Potter, and character and Toby mugs, with discounts of 20 to 70 percent. Bridal registry and a collector's club are added services.

Royal Knitting Mills Outlet

Manufacturers of rugged, high-quality sweaters and accessories in wool, wool blends, cotton, and acrylic, in assorted styles and colors, for children, ladies, men, and big and tall. The mills sell to outdoor wear catalogs; their outlet sells direct to the public at discounts of 50 to 70 percent.

Ruff Hewn

Rugged, comfortable sportswear for men and women who lead an active life-style, with savings of 35 to 50 percent.

Russell

Family sports apparel at 30 to 50 percent off.

S & K Famous Brands

Famous-brand men's suits include Botany 500, Tailors Row, Fenzia, Burt Pulitzer, Pierre Cardin, and many more. Also men's slacks, shirts, ties, and accessories.

Sara Lee Bakery

Delicious baked goods and pastries from the nationally known manufacturer.

Sassafras

Housewares, gifts, and contemporary life-style products for adults and children at savings of 10 to 50 percent.

Schuette Factory Outlet

Mirror brand first-quality and irregular cookware and bakeware. Foley mills, West Bend, and Empire electric appliances, Nesco roasters, and cookbooks are all brought to you at factory-direct prices.

Sears Outlet/Surplus

Savings of 20 to 70 percent off most original catalog and retail prices every day. Clearance, overstock, and discontinued merchandise for home and family, including clothing, housewares, electronics, furniture, and more.

Secaucus Handbag Outlet
Handbags, wallets, and accessories from famous manufacturers such as Stone Mountain, Esprit, Brio, Lauvier, and Barganza.

Sequels Book Outlet
Publisher closeouts discounted 50 percent or more. Selections include children's, fiction, cooking, travel, and a variety of other books. Something for everyone.

Sergio Tacchini
Proline first-quality tennis and golf wear for men, women, and children at savings of 20 to 50 percent off retail. Todd 1 and Cross Fusion sportswear also sold.

Shapely Factory Store
Classic Leslie Fay blouses, dresses, knitwear, and sportswear in a range of sizes, including petite and plus, at savings of 30 to 50 percent.

Sherwood Coats of Ohio
Direct from the factory in Alliance, Ohio, first-quality and irregular ladies' Sherwood, J. Hillery, and Travelers outerwear is sold with a savings of 20 to 40 percent.

Shoe Cents
First-quality, brand-name buy-outs from major department stores. Women's athletics and boots and men's shoes are $40 or less; women's dress and casual shoes are $20 or less.

Shoe Manufacturers Outlet
"The Best Brand at the Best Price" shoes for the entire family. All sizes available plus special orders.

Shoe Sensation
Shoe values for the entire family. Leading brands in a large selection of styles.

Shoe Stop Outlet Store
Discounted first-quality and buy-out ladies' designer shoes featuring

name brands such as Aigner, Van Eli, Naturalizer, Enzo, and more. The store carries sizes 4 to 12.

Side-Out
Discounts from 30 to 75 percent on unisex volleyball sportswear, sunglasses, sports bags, and volleyballs.

Silkcorp
Silk plants and trees.

Simandl Coat Factory
This manufacturer of first-quality, pure wool ladies' coats offers discounts of up to 60 percent off retail prices right at the factory. Hundreds of coats are stocked. Custom-made coats are available in any style or fabric in stock, cut to any length or sleeve length.

Sizes Unlimited
First-quality apparel for full-figure women in sizes 14 to 32.

Skyr
Skyr and Catcher sweaters, turtlenecks, and coordinated sportswear at 40 percent off.

Smoler Brothers Outlet
Direct from the manufacturer, with labels removed, are better ladies' fashions. Savings start at 20 percent off for first-quality items. Samples, seconds, closeouts, test runs, and discontinued and end-of-season merchandise can be discounted up to 50 percent.

Sneakers 'n Cleats
Men's, women's, and children's athletic shoes.

Socks Galore/Socks Galore and More
A sock-lover's dream come true. Over 60,000 pairs of designer dress, sport, tube, and slouch socks for the entire family, priced at 25 to 80 percent off retail. Brand names include Ann Klein, Christian Dior, Camp, Hue, and more.

Sony Factory Outlet Center
Sony electronics for less.

Specials Exclusively by Levi's
Levi Strauss and Company fashions for men, women, and children. Dockers, 501s, women's 900 series, jean jackets, and much more are 50 percent off the ticketed price.

Spiegel Outlet
Catalog overstocks as well as other merchandise.

Sports Authority
Sporting goods and fashions including team clothing and hunting, camping, fishing, biking, baseball, basketball, tennis, and other sporting equipment.

Sports Factory
Licensed college and major-league team logo sports apparel.

Sportsland USA
Sports souvenirs and apparel.

Sports Wearhouse
Family athletic clothing at discounts of 30 to 60 percent. Logo sweats of ABA, NFL, NCAA, NHL, colleges, and Disney characters. Brand names such as Chalk Line, McGregor, OP, and O'Neill.

Star Baby
Boys' and girls' clothing from Star Baby and What If in girls' sizes newborn to 6x and boys' sizes newborn to 7.

Stone Mountain Handbags
Top-quality leather goods from the manufacturer of Stone Mountain, Saddle River, and Ande lines. Discounts on handbags, travel bags, and accessories of 20 to 70 percent.

Supermarket of Shoes
Shoes of every kind—dress, casual, and athletic—and boots. Featured

brand names include Reebok, Jacqueline, Mushrooms, Nunn Bush, French Shriner, and more.

Susan Powter Fitness Outlet
Complete line of Susan Powter workout apparel for women of all sizes.

Swank
Extensive selection of men's and women's jewelry, personal leather goods, belts, fragrances, gifts, and personal accessory items. Lines include Swank, Pierre Cardin, Alexander Julian, Royal Copenhagen, Anne Klein, and Richard Scott, at 40 to 70 percent off.

Sweatshirt Company
Family apparel and activewear at 30 to 40 percent off. Mix-and-match styles and colors. Sizes for the whole family, including big and tall for men and plus sizes for women.

Swiss Miss
First-quality embroidered fabrics and laces suited for bridal and fine formal apparel, available directly from the factory. Discounts range from 20 to 50 percent.

Sycamore
Women's moderate casual apparel with well-known labels, such as Bill Blass jeans, My Michele, Options, Signet dresses, and more, always at a discount.

Tahari
Fine silk women's blouses, dresses, suits, and separates from the manufacturer.

Talbots
Ladies' fine classic clothes and accessories.

Tall Girls Outlet
Casual and dress clothing for tall women.

Tanner
Dresses, sportswear, casualwear, and activewear for women at this

factory-owned and -operated store. Look for discounts of 30 to 75 percent on Tanner, Tanner Sport, Doncaster, and Tanner Country labels.

Temptations Jewelry
Designer pieces to everyday wear in 14-Karat gold, sterling silver, and marcasite. A full line of accessories—scarves, belts, handbags, and sunglasses—to compliment your wardrobe.

This End Up Outlet
This End Up furniture and home accessories.

Thorngate Slack Outlet
A division of Hart, Schaffner & Marx. This outlet carries imperfect, name-brand, U.S.A.-made men's dress and casual slacks plus some shirts.

Ties, Etc.
Save 50 percent or more on a large selection of quality neck wear. You'll recognize famous brands like Givenchy, Liberty, and Brown & Church. Headquarters for hard-to-find extra-long ties, clip-ons, bow ties, and boys' ties, plus belts and suspenders.

Tiffany Factory Outlet
"Tiffany style" hand-leaded, stained glass lamps are discounted up to 40 percent.

Tool Warehouse
Great buys on hand tools of every description for the home, car, shop, garden, or farm. Hundreds of quality tools to choose from, all at truckload prices.

Top of the Line Cosmetics
Save on designer and brand-name cosmetics and fragrances from 25 to 75 percent off retail. Gift sets, makeup brushes, skin care products, and travel bags are also part of the large inventory. Trained consultants provide color analysis and makeup advice.

totes/Sunglass World
The weather protection experts save you 50 to 75 percent on umbrellas,

raincoats, rain hats, folding luggage, rubber boots, sunglasses, and more. The outlet features overstocks, closeouts, and select irregulars.

Towel Factory Outlet Center
Linens, towels, sheets, and other items for bed and bath at low, low prices. Expect to find a mix of first-quality, second-quality, irregular, and buy-out goods from manufacturers such as Cannon, Martex, St. Mary's, J. P. Stevens, and Royal Pacific.

Toy Liquidators
A wide selection of name-brand toys from Hasbro, Fisher-Price, Mattel, Playskool, and more, discounted up to 70 percent off suggested retail. Many are overstocks, package changes, and discontinued items. Some are less than manufacturers' original wholesale prices.

Toys Unlimited
New goods arrive daily at this discounter of nationally advertised, top-quality, name-brand toys. Savings can be as high as 75 percent off retail.

Trader Kids *see* Boston Trader Kids

Trend Club
Juniors' and misses' casual fashions and accessories.

Trophy Nut Store
In front of the 85,000-square-foot nut factory, nut products, mixes, and candies are sold in bulk or in one-pound packages at prices considerably less than retail.

Underwriters Recovery Sales Outlet
Anything and everything tested by Underwriters Laboratory. Inventory changes daily. Merchandise is mostly first quality, with some seconds, irregulars, and buy-outs. Expect discounts from 30 to 70 percent off retail. Get here early. Customers begin lining up one hour prior to the 10:00 A.M. opening.

Unisa
Quality handbags and shoes for women by Unisa.

Value Center

A variety of first-quality and slightly irregular family sportswear and outerwear is discounted 30 to 70 percent off manufacturers' suggested retail prices. Levi, Lee, Cotler, Jordache, JouJou, Esprit, Union Bay, and London Fog are among the many famous brand-names available.

Van Heusen

First-quality, current season men's and women's fashion apparel from the manufacturer at value prices. Savings of 20 to 60 percent on Van Heusen, Geoffrey Beene, Lady Van Heusen, and Aigner.

Vermillion Factory Outlet

Quality ceramic housewares and wood furniture for your home, direct from the factory.

VF Factory Outlet

From America's largest apparel manufacturer come first-quality Lee jeans, Health-Tex children's togs, Jantzen swimwear, Vanity Fair lingerie and sleepwear, Heron Cove Casuals, Kay Windsor dresses, and Bassett-Walker fleece wear for the entire family, at 50 percent off the ticketed price. Irregulars are ticketed and save you even more.

Village Clock Shop

Grandfather, wall, and mantel clocks, all first-quality from noted manufacturers such as Ridgeway, Howard Miller, and Sligh. Discounts are 30 to 50 percent of retail prices. Pulaski Furniture curios and accent pieces are also stocked. Free statewide delivery and shipping nationwide.

Villeroy & Boch

Fine china, dinnerware, flatware, gourmet ware, crystal, and giftware with the Villeroy & Boch, Wilkens, Asta, and Gallo brands at a 35 to 70 percent discount.

Waccamaw Pottery

Hard-to-beat discount prices on a tremendous selection of dinnerware, housewares, dried and silk flowers (loose or in arrangements), craft items, and so much more. Goods are all first-quality, with name brands such as Mikasa, Libbey, Corning, and others. Discounts can be as much as 80 percent off department store prices.

Wallet Works
First-quality leather wallets, clutches, key cases, travel products, handbags, briefcases, and accessories are direct from the manufacturer. Find brand names such as Amity, Stone Mountain, East Pak, High Sierra, and Desa, plus briefcases, luggage, handbags, and travel gifts, all at 25 to 75 percent savings.

Walnut Bowl/Chicago Cutlery
Walnut bowls, serving utensils, clocks, frames, and serving accessories direct from the factory with discounts of 50 percent.

Warehouse of Leathers
First-quality men's and women's leather apparel and accessories. Expect discounts of 10 to 20 percent below suggested retail price. Look for jackets, coats, pants, skirts, and a selection of eel skin accesories. Special purchases and sale items can make discounts soar to 50 percent or more.

Warren Cheese Plant
The creators of Apple Jack cheese. Their specialty is ethnic cheeses such as Swiss, string, mozzarella, provolone, and others sold to wholesale restaurant and grocery accounts. Prices are considerably less than retail.

Watches-N-Stuff
More than 150 styles in fashion look-alike watches for men and women. These copycats mimic the look of Rolex, Gucci, and Seiko and are guaranteed for one year. A one-stop shop for watch needs, with watchbands, straps, batteries, and accessories, including the Lorus line of Mickey Mouse watches.

Wayside Workshop
Fine reproduction furniture and unique gifts. Unfinished furniture, woodenware, gift items, and more.

The Wear House
Samples, seconds, one-of-a-kinds, overruns, and damaged items of children's outerwear, sweaters, swimwear, and sportswear direct from an

international manufacturer. Sizes range from infants through size 14. Merchandise is usually 20 to 60 percent off retail.

Wegmann's Diamond and Jewelry Mart
Discounts of up to 75 percent on fine 14-Karat gold and estate jewelry. Services include custom design and repair.

Welcome Home
The store that makes your home beautiful. Featured brand names include Marion Yu, Country Lace, and Lasting Impressions. Choose from a wide selection of giftware, framed art, table linens and textiles, romantic lace items, fragrant scents for the home, dolls, candles, and more.

Wemco Factory Store
A fantastic selection of men's brand-name neck wear and classic sportswear from makers such as Resilio, Wembley, Je Suis, and Lord Ascot. Sportswear is 40 to 60 percent off and neck wear is discounted 60 to 80 percent.

West Bend Company Store
Complete line of the manufacturer's electrical appliances, coffee makers, fitness equipment, and more. Seconds, closeouts, and demonstrators that save you up to 50 percent.

Western Publishing Outlet/The Boat House
The publishers of "Little Golden Books" sell first-quality books, games, paper products, and household items at discounts up to 60 percent.

WestPoint Pepperell
Linens, apparel, and home-decorating accessories with brand names such as Attelier, J. P. Stevens, Mar-tex, Lady Pepperell, and Utica. Savings range from 20 to 70 percent.

Westport Ltd./Westport Woman
"Fashion . . . factory to you!" Top-quality labels, including Westport Ltd., Princeton Club, Atrium, and Milano, for the career woman. Shop from the large collection of suits, dresses, sportswear, and separates in sizes 4 to 14 as well as plus sizes at Westport Woman.

What A Deal
Name brands and designer fashions, most sold at $12 and under. Teen fashions from Guess?, Gap, and L. A. Gear to fashions for the professional woman and plus sizes.

What On Earth
First-quality, discontinued international apparel and gifts from the catalog.

Whistling Wings
The world's largest mallard duck hatchery offers fresh, frozen, and smoked mallards, quail, pheasant, turkey, and other wild game. Their products are found in the finest restaurants, gourmet food shops, and upscale stores like Neiman Marcus and Marshall Field. Prices are about 50 percent off retail.

Whitewater Gloves
Ski, casual, dress, work, and hunting gloves. Jeans, belts, and jackets are also featured.

Whiting Manufacturing Outlet
Direct from the factory, bath and linen products such as quilts, bedding, towels, curtains, sheets, blankets, pillows, and more.

Windsor Shirt Company
The better way to buy a better shirt. From the manufacturer to you, over 20,000 discounted men's dress and sport shirts in forty-eight sizes.

Winona Glove Sales
Dress and work gloves, purses, wallets, ski accessories, woolen caps, scarves, socks, and moccasins at savings of 50 percent and more.

Winona Knits
Sweaters, sweaters, and more sweaters in cotton, acrylic, wool, and wool blends for men, women, and children. High-quality, American-made sweaters that are guaranteed.

Woolrich
Outerwear the outdoorsman has been counting on for over 160 years.

World Bazaar
International importers of casual home furnishings, accessories, and gifts, specializing in wicker and rattan. A large selection at warehouse prices.

Zak's Confections
An outlet store for Frankenmuth Fudge, Zak's also features freshly made chocolates, brittles, saltwater taffy, and novelty candy items at 10 to 50 percent off the original price.

Zubaz
Fashionable, life-style apparel for casual and active people in either the Mainline brand or licensed products.

Illinois

Numbers in this legend correspond to the numbers on the accompanying map. The number to the right of each city or town name is the page number on which that municipality's outlets first appear in this book.

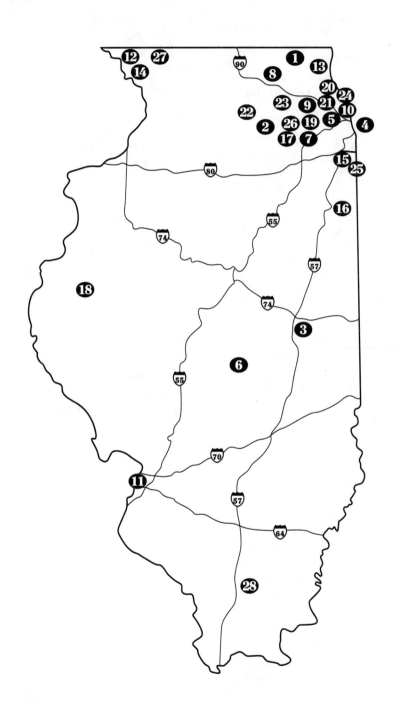

Antioch

Pickard Factory Outlet
782 Corona Avenue

Directions: I–94 to Rosecrans Road exit west (Route 173); proceed six miles to Route 83 and turn right; continue to Depot Street and turn right, then left at the next intersection (Corona Avenue); go around the bend and park in front of the Pickard Building.
Phone: (708) 395–3800
Hours: 8:30 A.M.–4:00 P.M., Monday–Saturday
Additional Savings: Seasonal and holiday sales plus monthly specials
Credit Cards: Discover, MasterCard, Visa
Personal Checks: Yes, with driver's license
Handicapped Accessible: Yes
Food: Nearly twenty fast-food stores and restaurants within a 2-mile radius
Bus Tours: Yes
Notes or Attractions: Display of hand-painted china created by Pickard craftsmen from 1893 to 1930 and sample of dinner service currently made for embassies, *Air Force One,* and other governmental/military agencies

Aurora

Misty Harbor
42 W. New York Street

Directions: I–88 to Route 31 south; proceed to Galena Boulevard; turn left onto Galena, travel 2 blocks to Stolp Avenue and turn left. Parking available at North Island Center on Stolp Avenue. Walk 1 block north to New York Street and turn left; store is 2 blocks to the west.
Phone: (708) 892–1828
Hours: 9:00 A.M.–4:30 P.M., Monday–Saturday
Additional Savings: Sales at the end of each season
Credit Cards: Discover, MasterCard, Visa
Personal Checks: Yes, with identification
Handicapped Accessible: Yes
Bus Tours: Yes, parking at North Island Center lot on Stolp Avenue

Lands' End Outlet Store
Yorkshire Plaza
4320 New York Street

Directions: Across from Fox Valley Mall; I–88 to Route 59 exit, then to Aurora Avenue (New York Street)
Phone: (708) 851–2990
Hours: 10:00 A.M.–9:00 P.M., Monday–Friday; 10:00 A.M.–6:00 P.M., Saturday; 11:00 A.M.–5:00 P.M., Sunday
Credit Cards: American Express, MasterCard, Visa
Personal Checks: Yes, with two forms of identification
Handicapped Accessible: Yes
Food: Available in shopping center vicinity

Champaign

Redwood and Ross Outlet
519 East Green Street

Directions: From I–74 take Lincoln Avenue exit south to Green Street.
Phone: (217) 344–0214
Hours: 9:00 A.M.–5:30 P.M., Monday–Saturday
Additional Savings: The "Big Sale" is held in March and August
Credit Cards: American Express, Discover, MasterCard, Visa
Personal Checks: Yes, with picture identification
Handicapped Accessible: Yes
Food: Many restaurants within 1 block
Bus Tours: Yes
Notes or Attractions: Within walking distance of the University of Illinois campus

Chicago

Adams Factory Shoe Outlet
3655–59 W. Irving Park Road

Directions: 1½ miles east of I–94 at the Route 19/Irving Park exit
Phone: (312) 539–4120

Hours: 9:00 A.M.–6:00 P.M., Monday–Saturday; 10:00 A.M.–4:30 P.M., Sunday
Additional Savings: Monthly sales and summer specials
Credit Cards: Discover, MasterCard, Visa
Personal Checks: Yes, with identification
Handicapped Accessible: Yes, with wide aisles and no steps
Food: Various restaurants within a 2-block area

Gabel's Discount Men's Wear
5719 N. Central Avenue

Directions: Take Kennedy Expressway (I–90) to Nagle Street exit; turn north (left), proceed to first light at Bryn Mawr Avenue, and make a right onto Central; approximately 2 blocks north on Central.
Phone: (312) 775–3171
Hours: 10:00 A.M.–6:00 P.M., Monday and Wednesday–Friday; 9:00 A.M.–5:00 P.M., Saturday; 10:00 A.M.–4:00 P.M., Sunday
Credit Cards: Discover, MasterCard, Visa
Personal Checks: Yes, with identification
Handicapped Accessible: Yes
Food: Restaurants and fast food available within 1 block
Bus Tours: No

Jefferson Industries Outlet Store
2100 South Marshall Boulevard

Directions: Take Sacramento exit off I–290, go right, and head south less than 2 miles; outlet will be on the right
Phone: (312) 277–6100
Hours: 9:00 A.M.–4:30 P.M., Monday–Saturday
Additional Savings: Weekly sales throughout the year
Credit Cards: Discover, MasterCard, Visa
Personal Checks: Yes, with proper identification
Handicapped Accessible: Yes, if accompanied by another person; six wide stairs in front of building
Food: Restaurant 1 block away
Bus Tours: Yes

Lands' End Outlet Store
Two locations within a block:
Women's store: 2241 N. Elston; (312) 384–4170
Men's store: 2317 N. Elston; (312) 276–2232

Directions: Kennedy Expressway to Fullerton Avenue; proceed to Elston Avenue, making a right; stores are on that block
Hours: 10:00 A.M.–6:00 P.M., Monday, Wednesday, Friday, and Saturday; 10:00 A.M.–7:00 P.M., Tuesday and Thursday; 11:00 A.M.–5:00 P.M., Sunday
Additional Savings: Weekly sales with additional markdowns of 20 to 40 percent
Credit Cards: American Express, Discover, MasterCard, Visa
Personal Checks: Yes, with two forms of identification
Handicapped Accessible: Yes, but ladies' store has two steps before entering. Sales associates will assist people in wheelchairs
Food: Fast-food on the block, sit-down restaurants within a 2-mile radius
Bus Tours: Yes

Mattress Factory, Inc.
2850 W. Irving Park Road

Directions: 1½ miles east of I–94 at the Route 19/Irving Park exit
Phone: (312) 478–1239
Hours: 9:00 A.M.–5:00 P.M., Monday–Saturday
Additional Savings: No
Credit Cards: Discover, MasterCard, Visa
Personal Checks: Yes, with a driver's license, state identification, or major credit card, plus name imprinted on checks
Handicapped Accessible: Yes
Food: Fast-food next door
Bus Tours: Yes

Meystel Warehouse
1222 S. Wabash Avenue

Directions: 4 blocks south of the Hilton hotel at Wabash and Roosevelt
Phone: (312) 347–3500

Hours: 10:00 A.M.–5:00 P.M., Monday–Friday; 10:00 A.M.–5:00 P.M., Sunday
Additional Savings: Sales in January and July
Credit Cards: All major cards
Personal Checks: Yes, with driver's license
Handicapped Accessible: Yes
Food: Around the corner
Bus Tours: Yes
Notes or Attractions: Near South Loop museum complex

Royal Knitting Mills Outlet
2001 S. California Avenue

Directions: In the southwest side of Chicago called Lawndale at Twentieth and S. California Avenue
Phone: (312) 247–6300
Hours: 8:30 A.M.–4:00 P.M., Monday–Friday
Credit Cards: MasterCard, Visa
Personal Checks: Yes, with proper identification
Handicapped Accessible: No
Food: Within 1 mile
Bus Tours: Yes, but call ahead for arrangements

Smoler Brothers Outlet
2300 W. Wabansia Avenue

Directions: 1 block north of North Avenue and 1 block east of Western Avenue
Phone: (312) 384–1200
Hours: 9:00 A.M.–4:00 P.M., Monday–Friday; 9:00 A.M.–3:00 P.M., Saturday
Additional Savings: Before Easter and Christmas sales
Credit Cards: MasterCard, Visa
Personal Checks: Yes, with proper identification
Handicapped Accessible: No, outlet located in basement level
Food: Cafeteria across the hall from outlet
Bus Tours: Yes
Notes or Attractions: Senior citizens on bus tours get an additional 10

percent discount. To qualify for discount, arrangements must be made ahead of time.

Cicero

Simandl Coat Factory
2506 S. Laramie Avenue

Directions: South of Eisenhower Expressway (Route 290) on Laramie Avenue
Phone: (708) 863–2718
Hours: 10:00 A.M.–4:00 P.M., Monday–Friday; 10:00 A.M.–2:00 P.M., Saturday
Additional Savings: Anniversary sale during July and August
Credit Cards: MasterCard, Visa
Personal Checks: Yes, with two forms of identification
Handicapped Accessible: No. Second floor walk-up
Food: Restaurants in the area
Bus Tours: Yes

Decatur

District Factory Outlet
125 E. North Street

Directions: ½ block east of Route 51 south and 1 block south of Route 36
Phone: (217) 422–6503
Hours: 10:00 A.M.–6:00 P.M., Monday–Thursday; 9:00 A.M.–6:00 P.M., Friday, 10:00 A.M.–5:00 P.M., Saturday (October through May)
Additional Savings: Sales held every two to three months
Credit Cards: MasterCard, Visa
Personal Checks: Yes, with driver's license
Handicapped Accessible: Yes
Food: All around downtown area within walking distance
Bus Tours: Yes

Downers Grove

Towel Factory Outlet Center
1730 Ogden Avenue

Directions: Call ahead
Phone: (708) 852–3616
Hours: 9:30 A.M.–9:00 P.M., Monday and Thursday; 9:30 A.M.–6:00 P.M., Tuesday, Wednesday, and Friday; 9:30 A.M.–5:30 P.M., Saturday; 11:00 A.M.–5:00 P.M., Sunday
Additional Savings: Month-long sale of select items
Credit Cards: MasterCard, Visa
Personal Checks: Yes, with driver's license and major credit card
Handicapped Accessible: Yes
Food: Available in the vicinity
Bus Tours: Yes

The Wear House
1404 Butterfield

Directions: On Butterfield at Finley just off I–88 at Highland Avenue
Phone: (708) 629–1282
Hours: 10:00 A.M.–8:00 P.M., Monday, Thursday, Friday; 10:00 A.M.–6:00 P.M., Tuesday, Wednesday, Saturday; 11:00 A.M.–5:00 P.M., Sunday
Additional Savings: Off-season sale three times a year
Credit Cards: MasterCard, Visa
Personal Checks: Yes, with proper identification
Handicapped Accessible: Yes
Food: A restaurant in mall
Bus Tours: Yes

East Dundee

Haeger Potteries Outlet
South Van Buren Street

Directions: I–90 to Route 25, exiting at Elgin; go north to Route 72 and west to the second stop light, Van Buren Street. Outlet complex 2 blocks south.

Phone: (708) 426–3441

Hours: 8:30 A.M.–5:00 P.M., Monday–Friday; 10:00 A.M.–5:00 P.M., weekends and holidays

Additional Savings: Annual tent sale from late June through mid-July

Credit Cards: MasterCard, Visa

Personal Checks: Yes, with two forms of identification

Handicapped Accessible: Yes

Food: Restaurants and fast-food as close as 2 blocks away

Bus Tours: Yes

Notes or Attractions: Free factory tours arranged by calling (312) 426–3441

Milk Pail Village Factory Outlet Stores
14 N. 630 Route 25

Directions: In Fox River Valley on Route 25, ¼ mile north of I–90

Phone: (708) 742–5043

Hours: 10:00 A.M.–8:00 P.M., Tuesday–Saturday; 10:00 A.M.–6:00 P.M., Sunday and Monday

Stores: (Partial listing; not all stores are outlets)

Bass Shoes

Houseware Outlet

Misty Harbor

Temptations Jewelry

Van Heusen

Credit Cards: Most stores take major credit cards

Personal Checks: Most stores accept personal checks with proper identification

Handicapped Accessible: Yes

Food: Restaurant adjacent to mall

Notes or Attractions: Located in beautiful, rural setting. Wildlife often seen from restaurant.

Elk Grove

Towel Factory Outlet Center
2404 E. Oakton

Directions: Call ahead
Phone: (708) 981–1620
Hours: 9:30 A.M.–9:00 P.M., Monday and Thursday; 9:30 A.M.–6:00 P.M., Tuesday, Wednesday, and Friday; 9:30 A.M.–5:00 P.M., Saturday; 11:00 A.M.–5:00 P.M., Sunday
Additional Savings: Month-long sale of select items
Credit Cards: MasterCard, Visa
Personal Checks: Yes, with driver's license and major credit card
Handicapped Accessible: Yes
Food: Available in the vicinity
Bus Tours: Yes

Evanston

Lands' End Outlet/Not Quite Perfect stores
816½ Church Street

Directions: Near the intersection of Church and Benson streets
Phone: (708) 328–3009
Hours: 10:00 A.M.–8:00 P.M., Monday and Thursday; 10:00 A.M.–6:00 P.M., Monday, Wednesday, Friday, and Saturday; 11:00 A.M.–5:00 P.M., Sunday
Credit Cards: American Express, MasterCard, Visa
Personal Checks: Yes, with two forms of identification
Handicapped Accessible: Yes

Fairview Heights

Shoe Stop Outlet Store
525 Lincoln Highway in Plaza St. Clair

Directions: From I–64 take State Highway 159 south through two traffic lights to Lincoln Highway; turn left and go ¼ mile to Plaza St. Clair

Phone: (314) 632–8909
Hours: 10:00 A.M.–8:30 P.M., daily
Additional Savings: Clearance sales at the end of each season in June and January
Credit Cards: American Express, Discover, MasterCard, Visa
Personal Checks: Yes, preprinted checks with valid driver's license. No starter checks.
Handicapped Accessible: Yes
Bus Tours: Yes

Galena

Capezio Shoes
113 North Main Street

Directions: On Main Street, several blocks off Route 20
Phone: (815) 777–1255
Hours: 9:00 A.M.–5:00 P.M., Monday–Sunday, with additional hours seasonally
Additional Savings: Special sales year-round
Credit Cards: American Express, Discover, MasterCard, Visa
Personal Checks: Yes, with proper identification
Handicapped Accessible: Yes
Food: Within 2 blocks
Bus Tours: Yes
Notes or Attractions: Galena is a historic town known for its Victorian architecture, antique shops, bed and breakfast inns, and Ulysses S. Grant historic sites

London Fog
113 North Main Street

Directions: On Main Street, several blocks off Route 20
Phone: (815) 777–9670
Hours: 9:00 A.M.–5:00 P.M., Monday–Sunday, with additional hours seasonally
Additional Savings: Special sales year-round

Credit Cards: MasterCard, Visa
Personal Checks: Yes, with proper identification
Handicapped Accessible: Yes
Food: Within 2 blocks
Bus Tours: Yes

Winona Knits
224 S. Main Street

Directions: On Main Street, 3 blocks off Route 20
Phone: (815) 777–2026
Hours: 9:00 A.M.–5:00 P.M., Monday–Sunday, with additional hours seasonally
Additional Savings: Weekly sales year-round
Credit Cards: MasterCard, Visa
Personal Checks: Yes, with proper identification
Handicapped Accessible: Yes
Food: On the same block
Bus Tours: Yes

Gurnee

Gurnee Mills
I–94 at I–32

Directions: Take I–94 and exit at Route 132/Grand Avenue, just past Great America theme park
Phone: (708) 263–7500 or (800) YES–SHOP
Hours: 10:00 A.M.–9:00 P.M., Monday–Saturday; 11:00 A.M.–6:00 P.M., Sunday
Stores:
Aca Joe
Air Step/Buster Brown
Ann Taylor Clearance Center
The Answer
Athlete's Foot Outlet
Bally

Banister Shoes
Bed, Bath & Beyond
Bermans Leather Outlet
Bigsby and Kruthers
Book Warehouse
Bostonian Hanover
Brass Factory Outlet
Brooks Fashion Company Store
Bugle Boy Outlet
Burlington Shoes
Camelot Music Outlet
Cape Isle Knitters
Capers
Capezio Shoes
Card and Gift Outlet
Carter's Childrenswear
Casual Male Big & Tall
Champs Outlet
Chico's
Cirage
Class Perfume
Clothestime
Colours by Alexander Julian
Corning/Revere
Cory Everson Fitness Fashions
County Seat
Dicken's Books
Dress Barn
Etienne Aigner
Famous Brands Housewares
Famous Footwear
Filene's Basement
Finish Line
Florsheim
Garage Outlet
Geoffrey Beene
Group USA
Guess?

Handbag Company Outlet
He-Ro Group
Jockey
Jonathan Logan
Just Sunglasses/Sunshade Optique
Kids Mart
Knot Shop
Lands' End Outlet Store
L'eggs/Hanes/Bali
Lingerie Factory
Littman Brothers
London Fog
Macy's Close-Out
Marshalls
Merry Go Round Outlet
Mondi
9 West
No Name Outlet
No Nonsense & More
Oak Leather
Oriental Weavers
Paper Factory
Perfumania
Polly Flinders
Prestige Fragrance & Cosmetics, Inc.
Publishers Outlet
Radio Shack
Remington
Route 66
S & K Famous Brands
Sears Outlet/Surplus
Secaucus Handbag Outlet
Sergio Tacchini
Silkcorp
Specials Exclusively by Levi's
Spiegel Outlet
Sports Authority
Star Baby

Susan Powter Fitness Outlet
Tahari
Tall Girls Outlet
This End Up Outlet
Tiffany Factory Outlet
Tool Warehouse
Top of the Line Cosmetics
Toy Liquidators
Trend Club
Unisa
Van Heusen
Wemco Factory Store
Credit Cards: Most stores accept most major credit cards
Personal Checks: Most stores accept personal checks with proper identification
Handicapped Accessible: Yes
Food: Two food courts with nearly twenty food vendors
Bus Tours: Yes
Notes or Attractions: Lockers are available for minimal cost. Wheelchairs are obtainable at the Shopper Information Centers free of charge with a valid driver's license as security deposit. Strollers and carts can be rented at minimal cost.

Hanover

Whistling Wings
113 Washington Street

Directions: On Highway 34
Phone: (815) 591–3512
Hours: 9:00 A.M.–5:00 P.M., Monday–Friday; 9:00 A.M.–noon, Saturday
Personal Checks: Yes, with identification
Handicapped Accessible: No
Food: Within 1 block
Bus Tours: Yes
Notes or Attractions: 16 miles from Galena near Mississippi Palisades State Park, downhill skiing, and the Mississippi River

Hometown

Towel Factory Outlet Center
8729 S. Cicero

Directions: Call ahead
Phone: (708) 424–4866
Hours: 10:00 A.M.–9:00 P.M., Monday–Friday; 9:30 A.M.–5:30 P.M., Saturday; 11:00 A.M.–5:00 P.M., Sunday
Additional Savings: Month-long sale of select items
Credit Cards: MasterCard, Visa
Personal Checks: Yes, with driver's license and major credit card
Handicapped Accessible: Yes
Food: Available in the vicinity
Bus Tours: Yes

Kankakee

Graham Industries Home Furnishings
200 N. Chestnut Street

Directions: I–57 to exit 312 west (Court Street); continue on Court to Schuyler Avenue and turn right; outlet is at first light, located in the Graham Industries factory building.
Phone: (815) 932–0008
Hours: 10:00 A.M.–5:00 P.M., Monday–Friday; 9:00 A.M.–3:00 P.M., Saturday
Additional Savings: No
Credit Cards: MasterCard, Visa
Personal Checks: Yes, with photo identification
Handicapped Accessible: Yes
Food: Restaurants and fast food within 1½ miles
Bus Tours: Yes, with advance notice

Lombard

Lands' End Outlet/Combo/Not Quite Perfect stores
Yorktown Convenience Center
Butterfield and Highland roads

Directions: exit I–88 at Highland Road
Phone: (708) 953–8855
Hours: 10:00 A.M.–9:00 P.M., Monday–Friday; 10:00 A.M.–6:00 P.M., Saturday; 11:00 A.M.–5:00 P.M., Sunday
Credit Cards: American Express, MasterCard, Visa
Personal Checks: Yes, with two forms of identification
Handicapped Accessible: Yes
Food: Available in shopping center vicinity
Bus Tours: Yes

Macomb

Haeger Potteries Outlet
411 W. Calhoun Street

Directions: Near the intersection of routes 67 and 136
Phone: (309) 833–2171
Hours: 9:00 A.M.–5:00 P.M., Monday–Saturday; 10:00 A.M.–5:00 P.M., Sunday
Additional Savings: Merchandise on sale each week with additional discounts
Credit Cards: Discover, MasterCard, Visa
Personal Checks: Yes, with two forms of identification
Handicapped Accessible: Yes
Food: Fast-food and restaurants on routes 67 and 136, approximately 2–3 blocks from the outlet
Bus Tours: No
Notes or Attractions: Macomb is near Argyle Lake State Park and 50 miles from Nauvoo, Illinois, site of one of the largest early Mormon settlements

Melrose Park

Towel Factory Outlet Center
1511 W. North Avenue

Directions: Call ahead
Phone: (708) 343–6666
Hours: 10:00 A.M.–9:00 P.M., Monday–Friday; 9:30 A.M.–5:30 P.M., Saturday, 11:00 A.M.–5:00 P.M., Sunday
Additional Savings: Month-long sale of select items
Credit Cards: Most major cards with a $20 minimum purchase
Personal Checks: Yes, with driver's license and major credit card
Handicapped Accessible: Yes
Food: Available in the vicinity
Bus Tours: Yes

Morton Grove

Lands' End Outlet Store
6131 W. Dempster

Directions: I–94 to Dempster exit. On Dempster between Edens Expressway and Waukegan Road
Phone: (708) 470–0320
Hours: 10:00 A.M.–9:00 P.M., Monday–Friday; 10:00 A.M.–6:00 P.M., Saturday; 11:00 A.M.–5:00 P.M., Sunday
Credit Cards: American Express, MasterCard, Visa
Personal Checks: Yes, with two forms of identification
Handicapped Accessible: Yes
Food: Available in shopping center vicinity
Bus Tours: Yes

Niles

Towel Factory Outlet Center
7313 N. Harlem Avenue

Directions: Call ahead
Phone: (312) 792–1700
Hours: 9:30 A.M.–9:00 P.M., Monday and Thursday; 9:30 A.M.–5:00 P.M., Tuesday, Wednesday, Friday, and Saturday; 11:00 A.M.–5:00 P.M., Sunday
Additional Savings: Month-long sale of select items
Credit Cards: MasterCard, Visa
Personal Checks: Yes, with driver's license and major credit card
Handicapped Accessible: Yes
Food: Available in the vicinity
Bus Tours: Yes

St. Charles

The Piano Factory Outlet Mall
410 S. First Street

Directions: 3 blocks south of Route 64 on First Street
Phone: (708) 584–2099
Hours: 10:00 A.M.–9:00 P.M., Monday–Friday; 10:00 A.M.–6:00 P.M., Saturday; 11:00 A.M.–5:00 P.M., Sunday
Additional Savings: Most stores offer additional discounts for senior citizens on Tuesdays
Stores:
Aileen
American Tourister/Buxton
Aunt Mary's Yarns
Banister Shoes
Bass Shoes
Book Warehouse
Cape Isle Knitters
Carter's Childrenswear
Champion Hanes

Chicago Records
Claires Clearance
Corning/Revere
Denmark Imports
Factory Card Outlet
Gitano
Houseware Outlet
Jonathan Logan
Just Pants
Kitchen Collection
Leather Manor
L'eggs/Hanes/Bali
Manhattan Factory Store
Misty Harbor
Pfaltzgraff Collector's Center
Temptations Jewelry
Toy Liquidators
Van Heusen
What A Deal
Credit Cards: Most stores accept most major credit cards
Personal Checks: Most shops accept checks with two forms of identification
Handicapped Accessible: Yes
Food: Cafe located within the mall
Bus Tours: Yes
Notes or Attractions: On the scenic west bank of the Fox River; mall is housed in a renovated piano factory

Schaumburg

Lands' End Outlet Store
The Annex
251 W. Golf Road

Directions: Near the intersection of routes 58 (Golf Road) and 72 (Higgins Road)
Phone: (708) 884–1900

Hours: 10:00 A.M.–9:00 P.M., Monday–Friday; 10:00 A.M.–6:00 P.M., Saturday; 11:00 A.M.–5:00 P.M., Sunday
Credit Cards: American Express, MasterCard, Visa
Personal Checks: Yes, with two forms of identification
Handicapped Accessible: Yes
Food: Near shopping center
Bus Tours: Yes

Meadows Town Mall
Golf and Algonquin roads

Directions: I–90 to Golf Road exit; continue to Algonquin Road
Phone: (708) 953–SAVE
Hours: 10:00 A.M.–9:00 P.M., Monday–Friday; 10:00 A.M.–6:00 P.M., Saturday; 11:00 A.M.–5:00 P.M., Sunday
Stores: (Partial listing; not all stores are outlets)
Bag & Baggage
Clothestime
Crown Jewels
Dress Barn/Dress Barn Woman
Factory Card Outlet
Famous Footwear
F & M Distributors
Hit or Miss
Kids Mart
Linens 'n Things
Loomcraft Home Decorating Fabrics
Waccamaw Pottery
Credit Cards: Most merchants accept major credit cards
Personal Checks: Most will accepted checks with a driver's license and major credit card
Handicapped Accessible: Yes
Food: Restaurants and fast food within the mall

Skokie

The Wear House
7136 Carpenter in the Village Crossing Shopping Center

Directions: Corner of Touhey and Carpenter between Edens Expressway (Route 94) and State Toll 294
Phone: (708) 933–1282
Hours: 9:00 A.M.–5:00 P.M., Monday–Wednesday and Saturday; 9:00 A.M.–8:00 P.M., Thursday and Friday; 11:00 A.M.–4:00 P.M., Sunday
Additional Savings: Off-season sales three times a year
Credit Cards: MasterCard, Visa
Personal Checks: Yes, with proper identification
Handicapped Accessible: Yes
Food: Restaurant in the mall
Bus Tours: Yes

South Chicago Heights

Oops We Goofed
18 East Sauk Trail

Directions: 3 miles west of I–394 on Sauk Trail
Phone: (708) 754–5250
Hours: 10:00 A.M.–5:00 P.M., Monday–Saturday
Additional Savings: March madness sale with additional 25 percent savings
Credit Cards: Discover, MasterCard, Visa
Personal Checks: Yes, with driver's license and credit card
Handicapped Accessible: Yes
Food: Eight restaurants within ½ mile
Bus Tours: Yes

Villa Park

J. C. Penney Outlet Store
250 W. North Avenue in North Park Mall

Directions: Take I–290 toward western suburbs; exit onto Highway 64.
Phone: (708) 279–1700
Hours: 9:30 A.M.–9:00 P.M., Monday–Friday; 9:30 A.M.–6:00 P.M., Saturday; 10:00 A.M.–5:00 P.M., Sunday
Additional Savings: Seasonal sales in May, June, December, and January
Credit Cards: American Express, J. C. Penney, MasterCard, Visa
Personal Checks: Yes, with proper identification
Handicapped Accessible: Yes
Food: Restaurants inside the mall and in mall lot
Bus Tours: Yes

Warren

Warren Cheese Plant
415 Jefferson Street

Directions: North of Route 20, a few blocks west of Highway 78
Phone: (815) 745–2627
Hours: 8:00 A.M.–4:00 P.M., Monday–Friday; 8:00 A.M.–noon, Saturday
Personal Checks: Yes, with identification
Handicapped Accessible: No
Food: Cafes on Main Street, which is 4 blocks away
Bus Tours: Yes
Notes or Attractions: Apple River Canyon State Park nearby; paddlewheeler river cruises are out of historic Galena, which is 30 miles away

West Frankfort

VF Factory Outlet Mall
1000 Factory Outlet Drive

Directions: I–57 to exit 65 at West Frankfort
Phone: (618) 937–3536 or (800) 772–VFFO
Hours: January through June 9:00 A.M.–7:00 P.M., Monday–Thursday; 9:00 A.M.–9:00 P.M., Friday and Saturday; noon–6:00 P.M., Sunday. July through December 9:00 A.M.–8:00 P.M., Monday–Thursday; 9:00 A.M.–9:00 P.M., Friday and Saturday; noon–6:00 P.M., Sunday.
Stores:
Banister Shoes
Bass Shoes
Bon Worth
Danskin Factory Outlet
Fieldcrest Cannon
London Fog
Paper Factory
Prestige Fragrance & Cosmetics, Inc.
Toy Liquidators
Van Heusen
VF Factory Outlet
Wallet Works
Credit Cards: Most stores accept major credit cards
Personal Checks: Most stores accept checks with proper identification
Handicapped Accessible: Yes
Food: Within the mall
Bus Tours: Yes

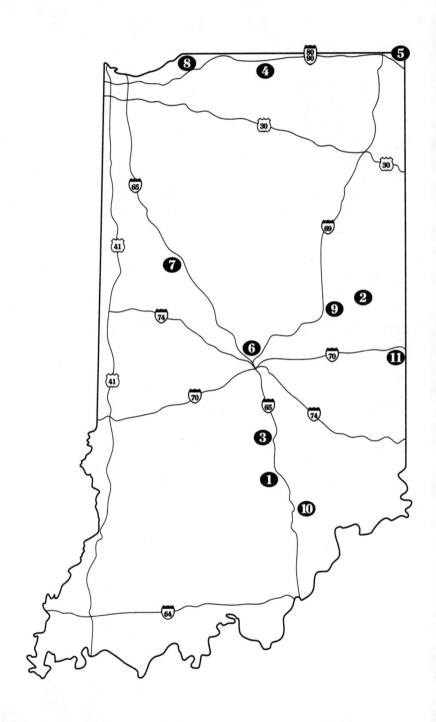

Indiana

Numbers in this legend correspond to the numbers on the accompanying map. The number to the right of each city or town name is the page number on which that municipality's outlets first appear in this book.

Columbus

Cosco Factory Outlet Store
2525 State Street

Directions: I–65 to Highway 46 east to Highway 7 south 4 miles
Phone: (812) 372–0141, extension 373
Hours: January–September 11:30 A.M.–5:00 P.M., Monday–Friday; October–December 10:00 A.M.–6:00 P.M., Monday–Friday; 10:00 A.M.–2:00 P.M., Saturday
Credit Cards: MasterCard, Visa
Personal Checks: Yes, with driver's license
Handicapped Accessible: Yes
Food: Local restaurants with wide selections of food within 1 mile
Bus Tours: Yes
Notes or Attractions: Columbus has unique architecture—over fifty public and private buildings by renowned designers and significant renovated historic structures

Dunkirk

Indiana Glass
1059 S. Main

Directions: State Road 67 north to 167 north. Turn left into outlet store at the factory.
Phone: (317) 768–7889
Hours: 10:00 A.M.–4:00 P.M., Monday–Saturday
Additional Savings: Sales during the Dunkirk Glass Festival (last weekend in May through first week in June)
Credit Cards: MasterCard, Visa
Personal Checks: Yes, with driver's license
Handicapped Accessible: Yes
Food: Drive-in across the street
Bus Tours: Yes
Notes or Attractions: Near Dunkirk Glass Museum, which has 3,000 pieces of glass from eighty-five factories. Museum open from May 1 through November l.

Edinburgh

Manufacturers Marketplace
11626 Executive Drive NE

Directions: On U.S. 31 at the I–65 junction; exit at 76B Edinburgh/
Columbus
Phone: (812) 526–9764 or (800) 866–5900
Hours: 10:00 A.M.–9:00 P.M., Monday–Saturday; 11:00 A.M.–6:00 P.M.,
Sunday
Stores:
Aileen
American Tourister/Buxton
Aunt Mary's Yarns
Banister Shoes
Barbizon
Bass Shoes
Black & Decker
Bon Worth
Book Warehouse
Brass Factory Outlet
Bugle Boy Outlet
Cape Isle Knitters
Corning/Revere
Evan Picone
Famous Brands Housewares
Fanny Farmer
Farah Factory Store
Farberware
Fieldcrest Cannon
Gitano
Hanes Activewear
Hush Puppies Factory Direct
Izod
Jonathan Logan
Kitchen Collection
Knits by K.T.
Leather Loft

L'eggs/Hanes/Bali
Maidenform
Old Mill Ladies Sportswear
Paper Factory
Pepperidge Farm
Perfumania
Ribbon Outlet, Inc.
Sara Lee Bakery
Sergio Tacchini
Socks Galore
Specials Exclusively by Levi's
Stone Mountain Handbags
Swank
Sweatshirt Company
Tool Warehouse
Toy Liquidators
Van Heusen
Wallet Works
Welcome Home
Westport Ltd.
Windsor Shirt Company
Zak's Confections

Credit Cards: Most merchants accept major credit cards

Personal Checks: Most merchants accept checks with two forms of identification

Handicapped Accessible: One-level shopping

Food: Food Court with a variety of hot foods and snacks; free indoor play area for kids located in Food Court

Bus Tours: Yes, discount coupons and shopping bags for tour participants

Notes or Attractions: Near Brown County State Park, Indiana's largest state park, and Columbus, famous for its art and architecture

Elkhart

Value Center
1333 S. Nappanee Street

Directions: 1 mile south of State Highway 20 on State Highway 19, which is ½ mile north of State Highway 33
Phone: (219) 293–0111, FAX (219) 293–2333
Hours: 10:00 A.M.–9:00 P.M., Monday–Saturday
Additional Savings: Winter and summer clearance held January, February, late August, and September; bargain basement and clearance rack available year-round
Credit Cards: Discover, MasterCard, Visa
Personal Checks: Local only (within 50 miles)
Handicapped accessible: Yes, with wheelchair accessible dressing rooms and rest rooms
Food: Fast-food within walking distance
Bus Tours: Yes
Notes or Attractions: Near Indiana Amish country. Elkhart is the recreational vehicle capitol of the country, with many manufacturers and van conversion companies located in town.

Fremont

Valley Outlet Center
655 W. State Road 120

Directions: 45 miles north of Fort Wayne, at the intersection of I–80/90 and I–69
Phone: (219) 833–1684
Hours: April through December 9:00 A.M.–8:00 P.M., Monday–Saturday; 11:00 A.M.–6:00 P.M., Sunday. January through March 9:00 A.M.–6:00 P.M., Monday–Friday; 9:00 A.M.–8:00 P.M., Saturday; 11:00 A.M.–6:00 P.M., Sunday
Stores:
Aileen
Aunt Mary's Yarns

Banister Shoes
Bass Shoes
Book Warehouse
Bugle Boy Outlet
Cape Isle Knitters
Carter's Childrenswear
Champion Hanes
Corning/Revere
Gitano
Hathaway
Hush Puppies Factory Direct
Izod
Jaymar
Kitchen Collection
Leather Manor
L'eggs/Hanes/Bali
Manhattan Factory Store
Old Mill Ladies Sportswear
Paper Factory
Socks Galore
Swank
Sweatshirt Company
totes
Toy Liquidators
Van Heusen
Welcome Home
Westport Ltd.
Credit Cards: Most merchants accept major credit cards
Personal Checks: Most merchants accept checks with two forms of identification
Handicapped Accessible: One-level shopping
Food: Pizza and snack shop on premises
Bus Tours: Yes
Notes or Attractions: Bank on premises. Mall near Pokagon State Park on the shores of Lake James, close to the Michigan border.

Indianapolis

Eastgate Consumer Mall
7150 E. Washington Street

Directions: Take the West Washington Street exit off I–465 ½ mile. Mall is on right side.
Phone: (317) 352–0951
Hours: 10:00 A.M.–9:00 P.M., Monday–Saturday; noon–5:00 P.M., Sunday
Additional Savings: Sidewalk clearance sales in second week of January and second week of July
Stores: (Partial listing; mall has both discount and retail stores)
Burlington Coat Factory Warehouse
Dr. Tavel's One Hour Optical
Elaine's
El-Bee Shoe Outlet
F & M Distributors
Famous Footwear
The Finish Line
Jewelies
Hit or Miss
Linens 'n Things
Old Mill Ladies Sportswear
Rosewood Galleries
Sizes Unlimited
Village Clock Shop
Credit Cards: Most stores accept major credit cards
Personal Checks: Most merchants accept checks with two forms of identification
Handicapped Accessible: Yes, with wheelchairs available
Food: Food court in the mall with a variety of snacks and foods.
Bus Tours: Yes

Lafayette

Lafayette Crossing
140 Frontage Road

Directions: I–65 at State Road 26 (Frontage Road)
Phone: None
Hours: 9:00 A.M.–9:00 P.M., Monday–Sunday
Stores:
Aileen
London Fog
Van Heusen
Welcome Home
Credit Cards: Most stores accept most major credit cards
Personal Checks: Most stores accept personal checks with proper identification
Handicapped Accessible: Yes
Food: Fast-food and restaurants on State Road 26 within 2 miles
Bus Tours: Yes
Notes or Attractions: Site of the Tippecanoe Battlefield, Wabash Heritage Trail, and Purdue University

Michigan City

Burnham Glove Factory Outlet
Wall Street

Directions: From I–94 exit onto 421 north; continue to Highway 20 at Marquette Mall. Left on Highway 20. At first light (Ohio Street) make a right. Travel to 1600 block. Look for grey sandstone building on the left with Burnham sign.
Phone: (219) 874–5205 or (800) 535–2544
Hours: 8:00 A.M.–4:00 P.M., Monday–Friday; Saturday 9:00 A.M.–3:00 P.M., from November through February 9:00 A.M.–noon, from March through October 1
Additional Savings: 10 percent off last two weeks in February
Credit Cards: MasterCard, Visa

Personal Checks: Yes
Handicapped Accessible: Yes
Food: 4 blocks away
Bus Tours: Yes
Notes or Attractions: Near Lighthouse Place Factory Outlet Mall, Lake Michigan, and Indiana Dunes

Hickey-Freeman
The Works, 711 Wabash Street

Directions: See directions for Lighthouse Place Outlet Center; The Works is an annex across the street
Phone: (219) 873–9051
Hours: 9:00 A.M.–8:00 P.M., Monday–Saturday; 10:00 A.M.–6:00 P.M., Sunday and holidays
Credit Cards: Most major cards
Personal Checks: Yes, with proper identification
Food: At Lighthouse Factory Outlet Center across the street
Handicapped Accessible: Yes
Bus Tours: Yes
Notes or Attractions: See Lighthouse Place Outlet Center

Lighthouse Place Outlet Center
Sixth and Wabash streets

Directions: From I–94 or Indiana Tollroad take Highway 421/Michigan City exit north to Sixth Street. Go left on Sixth Street to Lighthouse Place.
Phone: Visitor information (219) 879–6506; business office (219) 874–2915
Hours: 9:00 A.M.–8:00 P.M., Monday–Saturday, March through December; 9:00 A.M.–6:00 P.M., Monday–Saturday, January and February; 10:00 A.M.–6:00 P.M., Sunday
Additional Savings: Sidewalk sale last weekend in August and January warehouse sale
Stores:
Adolfo II
Adrienne Vittadini

Aileen
American Tourister/Buxton
Anko Also
Anne Klein
Aureus Factory Store
Avirex
Banister Shoes
Bass Shoes
Benetton
Boot Factory
Boston Trader Kids
Brands
Bugle Boy Outlet
Cape Isle Knitters
Capezio Shoes
Carole Hochman Lingerie
Carter's Childrenswear
Champion Hanes
Chaus
Chico's
Corning
Crystal Works
CW Company
Dansk
Donna Karan
Eagle's Eye
Eddie Bauer
Etienne Aigner
Famous Brands Housewares
Fieldcrest Cannon
Florence Eiseman
14 Plus Pizazz
Geoffrey Beene
Gitano
Guess?
harvé benard
Hathaway
Hush Puppies Factory Direct

Izod
Jaymar
J. Crew
JH Collectibles
Jockey
John Henry & Friends
Jonathan Logan
Jones New York
Jordache
Jordache Kids
Kitchen Collection
Leather Manor
L'eggs/Hanes/Bali
London Fog
Maidenform
Mark Cross
Multiples
Nickels Company Store
9 West
Oilily
Olga/Warner
Oneida
Paper Factory
Pepperidge Farm
Perfumania
Polo/Ralph Lauren
Prestige Fragrance & Cosmetics, Inc.
Remington
Ribbon Outlet, Inc.
Royal Doulton
Ruff Hewn
S & K Famous Brands
Sassafras
Side-Out
Specials Exclusively by Levi's
Socks Galore & More
Stone Mountain Handbags
Sweatshirt Company

Ties, Etc.
totes
Toy Liquidators
Van Heusen
Wallet Works
Welcome Home
Wemco Factory Store
Westport Ltd./Westport Woman
Credit Cards: Most major cards accepted
Personal Checks: Yes, with proper identification
Handicapped Accessible: Yes
Food: Restaurants and snack shops in Center
Bus Tours: Yes, with special discounts for groups
Notes or Attractions: Located close to the beaches of Lake Michigan, parks, a zoo, art galleries, museums, and the Indiana Dunes. An hour's drive from downtown Chicago.

Muncie

Indiana Glass Outlet
1300 Batavia Avenue

Directions: 12 miles east of I–69 on State Road 32
Phone: (317) 282–7047
Hours: 10:00 A.M.–6:00 P.M., Monday–Saturday; noon–5:00 P.M., Sunday
Additional Savings: During Dunkirk Glass Festival, last weekend in May through first week in June
Personal Checks: Yes, with driver's license
Handicapped Accessible: Yes
Food: Fast-food and restaurants nearby
Bus Tours: Yes
Notes or Attractions: Near Ball Canning Jar Museum, Ball State University Planetarium and Observatory, Minnetrista Cultural Center, and the Muncie Children's Museum (which displays a replica of Garfield the Cat)

North Vernon

Regal Rugs Factory Outlet
100 S. Madison Avenue

Directions: From the intersection where highways 3, 7, and 50 meet in North Vernon, go to the first stoplight and make a right. Outlet is ½ block farther on the left at the base of the telephone tower, 1 block from U.S. 50 and Indiana 7.
Phone: (812) 346–1555
Hours: 10:00 A.M.–5:00 P.M., Monday–Saturday
Credit Cards: Discover, MasterCard, Visa
Personal Checks: Yes, with proper identification
Handicapped Accessible: Yes
Food: Fast-food available 1 mile from store
Bus Tours: Yes
Notes or Attractions: Half an hour from Manufacturers Mall in Edinburgh and from Columbus, Indiana, known for its unique architecture. Forty-five minutes from Nashville, Indiana; Louisville, Kentucky; Cincinnati, Ohio; Indianapolis, and Brown County State Park.

Richmond

London Fog
3801 National Road East

Directions: From I–70 take exit 156A to 40 west; 2 miles farther, in Richmond Square Mall
Phone: (317) 966–1021
Hours: 10:00 A.M.–9:00 P.M., Monday–Saturday; 10:00 A.M.–5:00 P.M., Sunday
Credit Cards: MasterCard, Visa
Personal Checks: Yes, with two forms of identification
Handicapped Accessible: Yes
Food: Available in the mall
Bus Tours: Yes
Notes or Attractions: Near Nettle Creek Factory Outlet and outlet mall scheduled to open in summer 1994

Nettle Creek Factory Outlet
2200 Peacock Road

Directions: Take I–70 to Route 35 south. Turn left on Peacock Road. Outlet is several miles farther on the right side.
Hours: 9:00 A.M.–5:30 P.M., Monday–Friday; 9:00 A.M.–5:30 P.M., Saturday; noon–4:00 P.M., Sunday
Credit Cards: MasterCard, Visa
Personal Checks: Yes, with driver's license and major credit card
Handicapped Accessible: No ramp, two stairs to access main entrance. In some portions of the outlet aisles are tight for wheelchairs.
Food: On Route 35
Bus Tours: Yes

Iowa

Numbers in this legend correspond to the numbers on the accompanying map. The number to the right of each city or town name is the page number on which that municipality's outlets first appear in this book.

1. Chester 97
2. Iowa City 97

3. Story City 98
4. Williamsburg 99

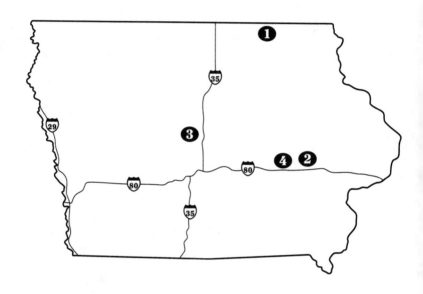

Chester

J & S Liquidators
Highway 63

Directions: On Highway 63 in downtown Chester, 1 mile from the Minnesota border
Phone: (319) 565–4065
Hours: 9:00 A.M.–7:30 P.M., Monday–Thursday; 9:00 A.M.–9:00 P.M., Friday–Saturday; 11:00 A.M.–6:00 P.M., Sunday
Additional Savings: August Crazy Days
Credit Cards: MasterCard, Visa
Personal Checks: Yes
Handicapped Accessible: By 1994
Food: Available in restaurants across the street
Bus Tours: Yes
Notes or Attractions: A historic brick building on the scenic upper Iowa River houses J & S Liquidators and a number of antique and craft shops

Iowa City

Lands' End Outlet Store
10 S. Clinton Street

Directions: From I–80 take the Dubuque Street exit south; turn right onto Iowa Avenue and left onto Clinton; outlet is on the left
Phone: (319) 338–2660
Hours: 10:00 A.M.–8:00 P.M., Monday and Thursday; 10:00 A.M.–6:00 P.M., Tuesday, Wednesday, Friday, and Saturday; noon–5:00 P.M., Sunday
Additional Savings: July, August, December, and January clearance sales with additional discounts of 20 to 40 percent
Credit Cards: American Express, Discover, MasterCard, Visa
Personal Checks: Yes, with proper identification
Handicapped Accessible: First floor only; second floor accessible only by a flight of steps
Food: A variety of restaurants and fast-food outlets on the same block
Bus Tours: Yes

Notes or Attractions: Across the street from the historic first capitol of Iowa and the University of Iowa

Story City

VF Factory Outlet
324 Factory Outlet Drive

Directions: I–35 to exit 124
Phone: (515) 733–5242 or (800) 772–VFFO
Hours: September through May 9:00 A.M.–7:00 P.M., Monday–Thursday; 9:00 A.M.–9:00 P.M., Friday–Saturday; noon–6:00 P.M., Sunday. June through August 9:00 A.M.–8:00 P.M., Monday–Thursday; 9:00 A.M.–9:00 P.M., Friday–Saturday; noon–6:00 P.M., Sunday.
Outlets:
Banister Shoes
Bass Shoes
Bon Worth
Danskin Factory Outlet
Famous Brands Housewares
Fieldcrest Cannon
Paper Factory
Prestige Fragrance & Cosmetics, Inc.
Toy Liquidators
Van Heusen
VF Factory Outlet
Wallet Works
Credit Cards: Discover, MasterCard, Visa
Personal Checks: Yes, with proper identification
Handicapped Accessible: Yes
Food: Available in the mall
Bus Tours: Yes

Williamsburg

Tanger Factory Outlet Center
Route 80

Directions: Take exit 220 off I–80 to Williamsburg
Phone: (319) 668–2811
Hours: 10:00 A.M.–9:00 P.M., Monday–Saturday; noon–5:00 P.M., Sunday
Stores:
Adolfo II
Aileen
American Tourister /Buxton
Barbizon
Bass Shoes
Black & Decker
Better Homes and Gardens Outlet
Boston Traders
Boston Trader Kids
Bugle Boy Outlet
Capezio Shoes
Cape Isle Knitters
Champion Hanes
Chaus
Corning/Revere
Crazy Horse
Etienne Aigner
Evan Picone/Gant
Famous Brands Housewares
Fieldcrest Cannon
Florsheim
Galt Sand
Geoffrey Beene
Gitano
harvé benard
Izod
JH Collectibles
Jordache
Jordache Kids

Kitchen Collection
L'eggs/Hanes/Bali
Leslie Fay
Liz Claiborne
London Fog
Maidenform
Mikasa Factory Store
9 West
Oneida Factory Store
OshKosh B'Gosh
Prestige Fragrance & Cosmetics, Inc.
Socks Galore & More
Swank
Toy Liquidators
Van Heusen
Wallet Works
Welcome Home

Credit Cards: Most stores accept major credit cards
Personal Checks: Most stores accept checks with proper identification
Handicapped Accessible: Yes
Food: Snack shop on the premises
Bus Tours: Yes
Notes or Attractions: Close to the historic Amana Colonies

Michigan

Numbers in this legend correspond to the numbers on the accompanying map. The number to the right of each city or town name is the page number on which that municipality's outlets first appear in this book.

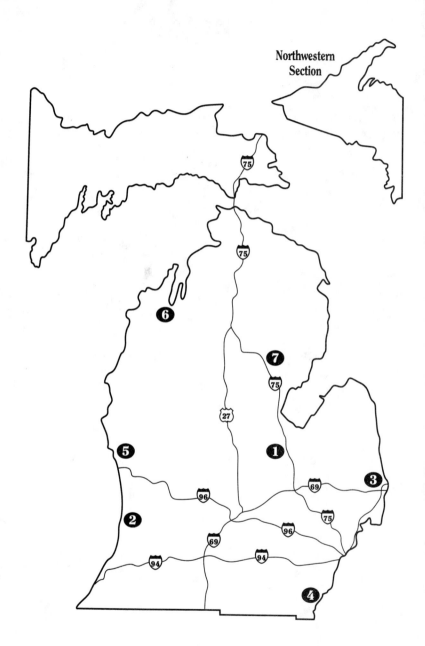

Birch Run

Manufacturers Marketplace
12245 South Beyer Road

Directions: Exit 136 Birch Run/Frankenmuth off I–75
Phone: (517) 624–9348 or (800) 866–5900
Hours: 10:00 A.M.–9:00 P.M., Monday–Saturday; 11:00 A.M.–6:00 P.M., Sunday
Stores: (Partial listing; specialty stores omitted)
Aileen
American Tourister/Buxton
Aunt Mary's Yarns
Banister Shoes
Barbizon
Bass Shoes
Black & Decker
Book Warehouse
Boston Trader Kids
Brass Factory Outlet
Bugle Boy Outlet
Cape Isle Knitters
Captree
Carter's Childrenswear
Champion Hanes
Columbia Sportswear
Corning/Revere
Dress Barn
Eddie Bauer
Esprit Direct
Fanny Farmer
Farah Factory Store
Farberware
Fashion Flair/Izod
Fieldcrest Cannon
Fuller Brush
Geoffrey Beene
Gitano

Hathaway
Helly-Hansen
Hush Puppies Factory Direct
Jewel Case
Jim & Chuck's Boot Outlet
Jockey
Jonathan Logan
Kid Spot
Kitchen Collection
Knits by K.T.
Langtry
Leather Manor
L'eggs/Hanes/Bali
Lenox
Manhattan Factory Store
Multiples
Newport Sportswear
Old Mill Ladies Sportswear
Oneida
OshKosh B'Gosh
Paper Factory
Perfumania
Pfaltzgraff Collector's Center
Pilgrim Silk Flowers
Polly Flinders
Remington
Ribbon Outlet, Inc.
S & K Famous Brands
Sara Lee Bakery
Sergio Tacchini
Skyr
Sneakers 'n Cleats
Socks Galore
Specials Exclusively by Levi's
Sportsland USA
Sports Wearhouse
Stone Mountain Handbags
Swank

Sweatshirt Company
Tool Warehouse
Top of the Line Cosmetics
totes/Sunglass World
Toy Liquidators
Van Heusen
Wallet Works
Welcome Home
Winona Knits
Zak's Confections
Credit Cards: Most stores accept major credit cards
Personal Checks: Most stores accept checks with two forms of identification
Handicapped Accessible: No
Food: Variety of snacks and foods in mall food court
Bus Tours: Yes
Notes or Attractions: Ten minutes from historic Frankenmuth and 7 miles from the world's largest Christmas store, Bronner's Christmas Wonderland

The Village Shops at Birch Run
12158 Beyer Road

Directions: Exit 136 Birch Run/Frankenmuth off I–75
Phone: (517) 624–4846 or (800) 969–3767
Hours: 10:00 A.M.–9:00 P.M., Monday–Saturday; 11:00 A.M.–6:00 P.M., Sunday
Stores:
Adolfo II
American Tourister/Buxton
Anne Klein
Brands
Bruce Alan Bags, Etc.
Capezio Shoes
Chaus
Eagle's Eye
E. J. Plum
Etienne Aigner

Evan Picone/Gant
Gilligan O'Malley
harvé benard
J. Crew
Jones New York
Jordache
Just Kids Outlet Store
Kitchen Place
Linen Mill
Liz Claiborne
Maidenform
Mikasa Factory Store
Nike
9 West
North Face
Prestige Fragrance & Cosmetics, Inc.
Sassafras
Villeroy & Boch
Welcome Home
Wemco Factory Store
Windsor Shirt Company
Credit Cards: Most stores accept major credit cards
Personal Checks: Most stores accept checks with two forms of identification
Handicapped Accessible: Yes
Food: Vending machines in lounge; food court at nearby Manufacturers Marketplace
Bus Tours: Yes

Holland

Manufacturers Marketplace Dutch Village
12330 James Street

Directions: I–196 to U.S. 31 at James Street
Phone: (616) 396–1808 or (800) 866–5900
Hours: 10:00 A.M.–9:00 P.M., Monday–Saturday; 11:00 A.M.–6:00 P.M., Sunday

Stores: (Partial listing; not all stores are outlets)
Action Homewares Outlet
Aileen
Ambassador Crystal
American Tourister/Buxton
Aunt Mary's Yarns
Banister Shoes
Barbizon
Bass Shoes
Black & Decker
Book Warehouse
Brass Town
Bugle Boy Outlet
Cape Isle Knitters
Carter's Childrenswear
Designer Brands Accessories
Dollar Discount Store
Dress Barn
Eddie Bauer
Evan Picone
Famous Footwear
Farah Factory Store
Fieldcrest Cannon
Fragrance Cove
Gitano
Hanes Activewear
harvé benard
Hush Puppies Factory Direct
Jockey
Jonathan Logan
Just About Perfect
Kid Port
Kitchen Collection
Leather Manor
Old Mill Ladies Sportswear
Oneida
Paper Factory
Pfaltzgraff Collector's Center

Ribbon Outlet, Inc.
Royal Doulton
Sergio Tacchini
Socks Galore
Sportsland USA
Sweatshirt Company
Toy Liquidators
Van Heusen
Wallet Works
Welcome Home
Winona Knits
Credit Cards: Most stores accept major credit cards
Personal Checks: Most stores accept checks with two forms of identification
Handicapped Accessible: Yes
Food: Food court
Bus Tours: Yes
Notes or Attractions: Hotel and theater located next to the mall. Marketplace is connected by a footbridge to Holland's Dutch Village. Windmill Island and the famous tulip gardens are minutes away. Close to Lake Michigan beaches.

Kimball

Manufacturers Marketplace
1661 Range Road

Directions: From I–94 take exit 269/Range Road
Phone: (313) 364–7001 or (800) 866–5900
Hours: 10:00 A.M.–9:00 P.M., Monday–Saturday; 11:00 A.M.–6:00 P.M., Sunday
Stores:
Aileen
American Tourister/Buxton
Banister Shoes
Bass Shoes
Book Warehouse

Bugle Boy Outlet
Cape Isle Knitters
Carter's Childrenswear
Champion Hanes
Corning/Revere
Fieldcrest Cannon
Izod
Leather Loft
L'eggs/Hanes/Bali
Paper Factory
Ribbon Outlet, Inc.
Socks Galore
Specials Exclusively by Levi's
Toy Liquidators
Van Heusen
Welcome Home
Westport Ltd./Westport Woman
Credit Cards: Most stores accept major credit cards
Personal Checks: Most stores accept personal checks with proper identification
Handicapped Accessible: Yes
Food: Eatery in the mall
Bus Tours: Yes, with discount coupons and shopping bags for prearranged bus tours
Notes or Attractions: On Lake Huron

Monroe

Manufacturers Marketplace
14500 LaPlaisance Road

Directions: I–75 to exit 11 north/LaPlaisance Road
Phone: (313) 241–9347 or (800) 866–5900
Hours: 10:00 A.M.–9:00 P.M., Monday–Saturday; 11:00 A.M.–6:00 P.M., Sunday
Stores: (Partial listing; not all stores are outlets or deep discounters)
Aileen

American Tourister/Buxton
Aunt Mary's Yarns
Banister Shoes
Barbizon
Bass Shoes
Book Warehouse
Brass Factory Outlet
Bugle Boy Outlet
Cape Isle Knitters
Carter's Childrenswear
Corning/Revere
Dress Barn/Dress Barn Woman
Evan Picone
Famous Brands Housewares
Famous Footwear
Farah Factory Store
Farberware
Fragrance World
Gitano
harvé benard
Jordache
Kitchen Collection
Knits by K.T.
Leather Manor
L'eggs/Hanes/Bali
Maidenform
Mikasa Factory Store
Multiples
Nike
Old Mill Ladies Sportswear
Paper Factory
Pepperidge Farm
Ribbon Outlet, Inc.
S & K Famous Brands
Socks Galore
Specials Exclusively by Levi's
Sportsland USA
Sports Wearhouse

Stone Mountain Handbags
Swank
Sweatshirt Company
Tool Warehouse
totes
Toy Liquidators
Trend Club
Van Heusen
Wallet Works
Welcome Home
Wemco Factory Store
WestPoint Pepperell
Credit Cards: Most stores accept major credit cards
Personal Checks: Most stores accept checks with two forms of identification
Handicapped Accessible: Yes
Food: Food court plus restaurants
Bus Tours: Yes
Notes or Attractions: Between Toledo and Detroit. Sterling State Park, the Henry Ford Museum, and Greenfield Village are near Detroit, and Cedar Point Amusement Park and Boblo Island are close to Toledo.

Muskegon

Outlets, Etc.
1940 Henry Street

Directions: From Business Route 131 go east on Laketon to Henry Street; outlets are between Laketon and Hackley
Phone: (616) 755–4604
Hours: 10:00 A.M.–9:00 P.M., Monday–Saturday; noon–5:00 P.M., Sunday
Stores: (Partial listing; not all stores are outlets)
Paper Factory
Kid Spot
Credit Cards: Most major cards
Personal Checks: Yes
Handicapped Accessible: Yes

Food: Cafe located in the mall
Bus Tours: Yes
Notes or Attractions: Beaches, three state parks, and two amusement parks are nearby

Traverse City

Manufacturers Marketplace
3639 Market Place Circle

Directions: Take U.S. 31 south of downtown Traverse City
Phone: (616) 941–9211 or (800) 866–5900
Hours: 10:00 A.M.–9:00 P.M., Monday–Saturday; 11:00 A.M.–6:00 P.M., Sunday
Stores:
Banister Shoes
Barbizon
Bass Shoes
Book Warehouse
Bugle Boy Outlet
Cape Isle Knitters
Carter's Childrenswear
Corning/Revere
Designer Brands Accessories
Eddie Bauer
Famous Brands Housewares
Fitz and Floyd
Geoffrey Beene
Gitano
Great Outdoor Clothing
Hush Puppies Factory Direct
Izod
Kitchen Collection
Leather Loft
L'eggs/Hanes/Bali
Paper Factory
Perfumania

Polly Flinders
Ribbon Outlet, Inc.
Russell
Socks Galore
Specials Exclusively by Levi's
Stone Mountain Handbags
Swank
Toy Liquidators
Van Heusen
Welcome Home
Westport Ltd.
Credit Cards: Most stores accept major credit cards
Personal Checks: Most stores accept personal checks with proper iden-
tification
Handicapped Accessible: Yes
Food: Restaurant in the mall
Bus Tours: Yes
Notes or Attractions: Near vacation area of Michigan, with seasonal
fishing, skiing, and golfing close by

West Branch

Tanger Factory Outlet Center
I–75 and Route 58

Directions: Take exit 212 off I–75
Phone: (517) 345–4437 or (800) 727–6885
Hours: 10:00 A.M.–9:00 P.M., Monday–Saturday; noon–6:00 P.M., Sunday
Stores:
Adolfo II
Barbizon
Bruce Alan Bags, Etc.
Cape Isle Knitters
Coach
Crazy Horse
Etienne Aigner
Gitano

harvé benard
John Henry & Friends
L'eggs/Hanes/Bali
London Fog
Maidenform
Pfaltzgraff Collector's Center
Reebok
Top of the Line Cosmetics
Van Heusen
Welcome Home
Credit Cards: Most stores accept major credit cards
Personal Checks: Most stores accept personal checks with proper identification
Handicapped Accessible: Yes
Food: Nearby
Bus Tours: Yes

Minnesota

Numbers in this legend correspond to the numbers on the accompanying map. The number to the right of each city or town name is the page number on which that municipality's outlets first appear in this book.

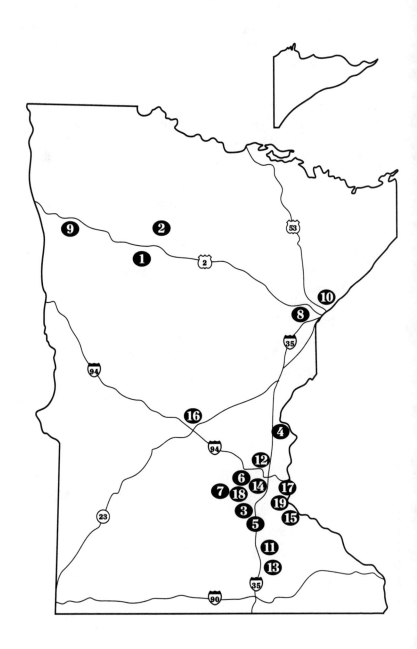

Bemidji

Bemidji Woolen Mills
301 Irvine Avenue NW

Directions: At Third Street and Irvine Avenue, 4 blocks west of the statues of Paul Bunyan and Babe the Blue Ox
Phone: (218) 751–5166
Hours: 8:00 A.M.–5:30 P.M., Monday–Saturday
Credit Cards: Discover, MasterCard, Visa
Personal Checks: Yes, with driver's license
Handicapped Accessible: Yes
Food: Within walking distance
Bus Tours: Yes, with a parking lot large enough for recreational vehicles
Notes or Attractions: Bemidji is the home of statues of Paul Bunyan and Babe the Blue Ox; Itasca Park, at the headwaters of the Mississippi River, is 50 miles north.

Lady Slipper Designs Outlet Store—The Gift Outlet
315 Irvine Avenue NW

Directions: At Third Street and Irvine Avenue in downtown Bemidji, 4 blocks west of the statues of Paul Bunyan and Babe the Blue Ox
Phone: (218) 751–7501
Hours: Memorial Day through December, 10:00 A.M.–5:30 P.M., Monday–Saturday
Additional Savings: Annual Christmas Sale Day; call for dates and hours
Credit Cards: MasterCard, Visa
Personal Checks: Yes, with identification
Handicapped Accessible: Yes
Food: Within walking distance
Bus Tours: Yes
Notes or Attractions: Bemidji is the home of Paul Bunyan and Babe the Blue Ox statues; Itasca Park, at the headwaters of the Mississippi River, is 50 miles north.

Blackduck

Anderson Fabrics Outlet Store
Box 311 Lake Road

Directions: North on U.S. 71 from Bemidji to Lake Road
Phone: (800) 638–8921
Hours: 9:00 A.M.–5:30 P.M., Monday–Friday; 9:00 A.M.–4:00 P.M., Saturday
Credit Cards: Discover, MasterCard, Visa
Personal Checks: Yes, with identification
Handicapped Accessible: Yes
Food: Within a block
Bus Tours: Yes
Notes or Attractions: Factory tour can be arranged by contacting store manager; near Chippewa National Forest; Bimidji is 25 miles south

Bloomington

Sears Surplus
9056 S. Penn Avenue

Directions: Take Ninetieth Street or Ninety-Fourth Street exit off Highway 35W for roughly 5 blocks west; 1 mile south of Southtown Shopping Mall
Phone: (612) 884–5317
Hours: 9:00 A.M.–9:00 P.M., Monday–Saturday; 11:00 A.M.–6:00 P.M., Sunday
Credit Cards: Discover and Sears
Personal Checks: Yes, with two forms of identification
Handicapped Accessible: Yes
Food: Fast-food next door
Bus Tours: Yes

Branch

Tanger Factory Outlet Center
I–35 North

Directions: Take I–35 north to exit 147 at Highway 95
Phone: (612) 674–5885
Hours: 10:00 A.M.–9:00 P.M., Monday–Saturday; 11:00 A.M.–6:00 P.M., Sunday
Stores:
Adolfo II
American Tourister
Bass Shoes
Boston Trader Kids
Brown Shoe Outlet
Bugle Boy Outlet
Cape Isle Knitters
Capezio Shoes
Carter's Childrenswear
Corning/Revere
Famous Brands Housewares
Geoffrey Beene
Kitchen Collection
L'eggs/Hanes/Bali
Leslie Fay
Liz Claiborne
Naturalizer
9 West
Reebok
Socks Galore & More
Toy Liquidators
Van Heusen
Welcome Home
Woolrich
Credit Cards: Most stores accept major credit cards
Personal Checks: Most stores accept personal checks with proper identification
Handicapped Accessible: Yes

Food: Nearby
Bus Tours: Yes
Notes or Attractions: 40 miles north of Minneapolis/St. Paul

Burnsville

Recie's Sample Shop
1930 Highway 13 East

Directions: Located on northwest corner of Highway 13 and Cliff Road. Call for directions.
Phone: (612) 882–1667 or (612) 882–1668
Hours: 10:00 A.M.–9:00 P.M., Monday–Friday; 10:00 A.M.–5:30 P.M., Saturday; noon–5:00 P.M., Sunday
Additional Savings: Seasonal sales after July Fourth and Christmas
Credit Cards: Discover, MasterCard, Visa
Personal Checks: Yes, with identification
Handicapped Accessible: Yes
Food: Yes, on the same block
Bus Tours: Yes

Chanhassen

Carousel Animal Fair Factory Outlet
581 W. Seventy-Eighth Street

Directions: Highway 5 west through Chanhassen center to Seventy-Eighth Street
Phone: (612) 934–0444
Hours: 10:00 A.M.–5:30 P.M., Monday–Wednesday, Friday, and Saturday; 10:00 A.M.–7:00 P.M., Thursday; noon–5:00 P.M., Sunday
Credit Cards: None
Personal Checks: Yes
Handicapped Accessible: Yes
Bus Tours: Yes
Notes or Attractions: Near Chanhassen Dinner Theater and University of Minnesota Landscape Arboretum

Chaska

Bubbles and Scents Factory Outlet
102 W. Fifth Street

Directions: 1 block south of Highway 212 and Highway 41
Phone: (612) 448–6900
Hours: 10:00 A.M.–5:30 P.M., Monday–Thursday; 10:00 A.M.–7:00 P.M., Friday; 10:00 A.M.–5:30 P.M., Saturday; open Sundays six weeks prior to Christmas
Additional Savings: Weekly in-store specials
Credit Cards: Discover, MasterCard, Visa
Personal Checks: Yes, with picture identification
Handicapped Accessible: Yes
Food: Yes
Bus Tours: Yes

Cloquet

Bergquist Imports, Inc.
1412 Highway 33 South

Directions: I–35W north to Highway 33. Follow to Cloquet; outlet is ½ mile from exit
Phone: (218) 879–1142
Hours: 9:00 A.M.–5:30 P.M., Monday–Saturday
Credit Cards: None
Personal Checks: Yes, with proper identification
Handicapped Accessible: Yes
Food: Restaurants and fast-food within a 1-mile radius
Bus Tours: Yes
Notes or Attractions: Cloquet is near Dunlop Island, which features a western fort and Indian village. Bergquist Imports has a gift shop on the premises that offers the largest selection of Scandinavian gift items in the United States.

Crookston

Anderson Fabrics
109 S. Broadway

Directions: U.S. 2 west from Bimidji to Crookston exit
Phone: (218) 281–1806
Hours: 9:30 A.M.–6:00 P.M., Monday–Wednesday and Friday; 9:30
A.M.–7:00 P.M., Thursday; 9:30 A.M.–4:00 P.M., Saturday
Credit Cards: MasterCard, Visa
Personal Checks: Yes, with identification
Handicapped Accessible: First floor only
Food: Within a block
Bus Tours: Yes
Notes or Attractions: Near scenic Red River Valley area

Duluth

Eddie Bauer
5115 Burning Tree Road in Burning Tree Plaza

Directions: Take Highway 53 north and turn left at Maple Grove Road;
turn right at Burning Tree Road and left into Burning Tree Plaza.
Phone: (218) 727–5502
Hours: 10:00 A.M.–9:00 P.M., Monday–Friday; 10:00 A.M.–6:00 P.M., Satur-
day; noon–5:00 P.M., Sunday
Credit Cards: American Express, MasterCard, Visa
Personal Checks: Yes, with proper identification
Handicapped Accessible: Yes
Food: In shopping center
Bus Tours: Yes
Notes or Attractions: Near Lake Superior, where water sports and year-
round outdoor activities are available

Faribault

Faribo Woolens
1819 Second Avenue NW

Directions: Take I–35 to Faribault then follow billboards.
Phone: (507) 334–1644
Hours: 9:00 A.M.–5:30 P.M., Monday–Saturday; noon–4:00 P.M., Sunday
Additional Savings: January and June clearances
Credit Cards: American Express, Discover, MasterCard, Visa
Personal Checks: Yes, with driver's license
Handicapped Accessible: Yes
Food: 1 mile away
Bus Tours: Yes
Notes or Attractions: Shipping and mail-order services available

Fridley

Sears Outlet/Surplus
1000 N.E. East Moore Lake Drive

Directions: Highway 65N to Central Avenue to Moore Lake Drive
Phone: (612) 571–8010
Hours: 9:00 A.M.–9:00 P.M., Monday–Saturday; 11:00 A.M.–6:00 P.M., Sunday
Credit Cards: Discover and Sears
Personal Checks: Yes, with two forms of identification
Handicapped Accessible: Yes
Food: Available in the area
Bus Tours: Yes

Medford

Medford Outlet Center
315 County Road 12 SW

Directions: Take exit 48 off I–35
Phone: (507) 455–4111
Hours: 10:00 A.M.–9:00 P.M., Monday–Saturday; 11:00 A.M.–6:00 P.M., Sunday
Stores:
Adolfo II
Bass Shoes
Cape Isle Knitters
Capezio Shoes
Chaus
Corning/Revere
Etienne Aigner
Famous Brands Housewares
Geoffrey Beene
Gitano
I. B. Diffusion
Jordache
Kitchen Collection
Leather Loft
L'eggs/Hanes/Bali
Liz Claiborne
Maidenform
Mikasa Factory Store
NCS Shoe Outlet
Nike
9 West
North Face
Perfumania
Ribbon Outlet, Inc.
Socks Galore
Toys Unlimited
Van Heusen
Welcome Home

Credit Cards: Most stores accept major credit cards
Personal Checks: Most stores accept checks with proper identification
Handicapped Accessible: Yes
Food: On premises
Bus Tours: Yes

Minneapolis

Dayton's Outlet Store
701 Industrial Boulevard

Directions: Take Highway 35 west to exit 22; proceed 2 blocks to Industrial Boulevard, close to Rosedale Mall
Phone: (612) 623–7111
Hours: 10:00 A.M.–9:30 P.M., Monday–Friday; 10:30 A.M.–6:00 P.M., Saturday; noon–6:00 P.M., Sunday
Credit Cards: American Express, Dayton's, Discover, MasterCard, Visa
Personal Checks: Yes, with driver's license or Dayton's charge
Handicapped Accessible: Yes
Food: In the vicinity
Bus Tours: Yes

Sears Outlet/Surplus
2700 Winter Street NE

Directions: Take Highway 35 west to Industrial Boulevard; proceed east to Winter Street
Phone: (612) 379–5600
Hours: 9:00 A.M.–9:00 P.M., Monday–Friday; 9:00 A.M.–5:00 P.M., Saturday; noon–5:00 P.M., Sunday
Credit Cards: Sears, Discover
Personal Checks: Yes, with two forms of identification and driver's license showing date of birth
Handicapped Accessible: Yes
Food: Within a few blocks
Bus Tours: Yes

Red Wing

Pottery Place Outlet Center
2000 W. Main Street

Directions: Withers Harbor Drive exit off Highway 61
Phone: (612) 388-1428
Hours: 9:00 A.M.–8:00 P.M., Monday–Friday; 9:00 A.M.–6:00 P.M., Saturday; 11:00 A.M.–6:00 P.M., Sunday
Stores:
Accessories Outlet
Aileen
Banister Shoes
Bass Shoes
Bouquet's of Red Wing
Corning/Revere
Faribo Woolens
Hush Puppies Factory Direct
L'eggs/Hanes/Bali
Paper Factory
Plums (Sweaters for Less)
Prestige Fragrance & Cosmetics, Inc.
Riverwoods Creations
United Colors of Benetton
Van Heusen
Wallet Works
Winona Glove Sales
Credit Cards: Most stores accept major credit cards
Personal Checks: Most stores accept checks with proper identification
Handicapped Accessible: Yes
Food: Two restaurants within the mall and one in an adjoining building
Bus Tours: Yes
Notes or Attractions: Mall is on the National Register of Historic Places. One hour south of Minneapolis/St. Paul. Red Wing is a mid–nineteenth-century Mississippi River town with restored historic buildings.

St. Cloud

Jennings Decoy Company
601 Franklin Avenue NE

Directions: Exit Highway 10 at the east St. Germain intersection and travel north 6 blocks on the Highway 10 west frontage road.
Phone: (612) 253–2253 or (800) 331–5613
Hours: 8:00 A.M.–5:00 P.M., Monday–Friday; 9:00 A.M.–3:00 P.M., Saturday
Credit Cards: Discover, MasterCard, Visa
Personal Checks: Yes, with driver's license
Handicapped Accessible: Yes
Food: Available 6 blocks away
Bus Tours: Yes

St. Paul

Milbern Clothing Company
Two St. Paul locations:

1685 University Avenue (Midway area); (612) 645–2922
Directions: Take I–94 to North Snelling Avenue to West University Avenue; the store is 2 blocks east of Snelling and University avenues.

Galtier Plaza, second floor (Milton Division); (612) 224–6443
Directions: Located in downtown St. Paul across from Mears Park

Hours: Midway: 9:00 A.M.–5:00 P.M., Tuesday, Wednesday, Friday, and Saturday; 9:00 A.M.–9:00 P.M., Monday and Thursday
Milton Division: 10:00 A.M.–7:00 P.M., Monday–Saturday; noon–5:00 P.M., Sunday
Additional Savings: Warehouse clearance; call for dates
Credit Cards: Discover, MasterCard, Visa
Personal Checks: Yes, with proper identification
Handicapped Accessible: Yes
Food: Available nearby

Shakopee

Bubbles and Scents Factory Outlet
1000 Valley Park Drive

Directions: ½ mile south of Valley Fair Amusement Park on Highway 101
Phone: (612) 496–4710
Hours: 9:30 A.M.–5:00 P.M., Monday–Saturday; open Sundays six weeks prior to Christmas
Additional Savings: Weekly in-store specials
Credit Cards: Discover, MasterCard, Visa
Personal Checks: Yes, with picture identification
Handicapped Accessible: Yes
Food: Yes
Bus Tours: Yes
Notes or Attractions: Located near Valley Fair Amusement Park and Mystic Lake Casino

Woodbury

Manufacturers Marketplace
10150 Hudson Road

Directions: From I–94 take exit 251 to County Road 19. Located fifteen minutes east of the Twin Cities.
Phone: (612) 735–9060 or (800) 866–5900
Hours: 10:00 A.M.–9:00 P.M., Monday–Saturday; 11:00 A.M.–6:00 P.M., Sunday
Stores:
Aileen
American Tourister/Buxton
Banister Shoes
Book Warehouse
Boston Trader Kids
Brown Shoe Outlet
Bugle Boy Outlet

Cape Isle Knitters
Eddie Bauer
Famous Brands Housewares
Fieldcrest Cannon
Geoffrey Beene
Izod
Jonathan Logan
Kids Express
Kitchen Collection
Leather Loft
L'eggs/Hanes/Bali
Paper Factory
Ribbon Outlet, Inc.
Sara Lee Bakery
Socks Galore
Specials Exclusively by Levi's
Toy Liquidators
Van Heusen
Welcome Home
Westport Ltd./Westport Woman
Winona Knits
Credit Cards: Most stores accept major credit cards
Personal Checks: Most stores accepts checks with proper identification
Handicapped Accessible: Yes
Food: Restaurant on premises
Bus Tours: Yes
Notes or Attractions: Located in the Stillwater area near recreational activities; Minneapolis and St. Paul are minutes away

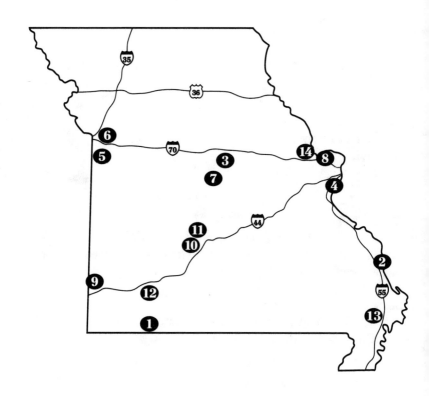

Missouri

Numbers in this legend correspond to the numbers on the accompanying map. The number to the right of each city or town name is the page number on which that municipality's outlets first appear in this book.

Branson

Factory Merchants Mall of Branson
1000 Pat Nash Drive

Directions: U.S. 65 to Highway 76 west in Branson. Take Shepard of the Hills bypass to Gretna Road.
Phone: (417) 335–6686
Hours: January and February 10:00 A.M.–6:00 P.M., daily; March to October 9:00 A.M.–9:00 P.M., Monday–Saturday; 9:00 A.M.–6:00 P.M., Sunday. November and December 9:00 A.M.–8:00 P.M., Monday–Saturday; 9:00 A.M.–6:00 P.M., Sunday
Stores:
Aileen
American Tourister/Buxton
Banister Shoes
Barbizon
Bass Shoes
Bon Worth
Book Warehouse
Boot Factory
Bruce Alan Bags
Bugle Boy Outlet
Cape Isle Knitters
Carter's Childrenswear
Champion Hanes
Corning/Revere
Etienne Aigner
Evan Picone
Famous Footwear
Farberware
Fashion Flair
Fieldcrest Cannon
Florsheim
Full Size Fashions
Geoffrey Beene
Gitano
Hush Puppies Factory Direct

Jaymar
Jonathan Logan
Kitchen Collection
Leather Factory
L'eggs/Hanes/Bali
London Fog
Manhattan Factory Store
Oneida
OshKosh B'Gosh
Pfaltzgraff Collector's Center
Prestige Fragrance & Cosmetics, Inc.
Rawlings
Ribbon Outlet, Inc.
Ruff Hewn
Socks Galore and More
totes
Toys Unlimited
Van Heusen
Vermillion Factory Outlet
Wallet Works
Walnut Bowl/Chicago Cutlery
Welcome Home
Credit Cards: Most major cards accepted
Personal Checks: Most merchants accept checks with two forms of identification
Food: Deli and sweet shop in the mall
Bus Tours: Yes; ample parking
Notes or Attractions: In Ozark Mountain country, a vacation getaway with attractions for the entire family

Cape Girardeau

Florsheim
48 South Plaza Way

Directions: From I–55 east take exit 96 to Kings Highway; turn left onto Independence and right into Plaza Way center

Phone: (314) 334–9544
Hours: 9:00 A.M.–5:30 P.M., Monday–Saturday; noon–4:00 P.M., Sunday
Credit Cards: American Express, Discover, MasterCard, Visa
Personal Checks: Yes; out-of-state residents need driver's license identification
Handicapped Accessible: Yes
Food: A variety of restaurants within 2 miles
Bus Tours: Yes

Thorngate Slack Outlet
637 Broadway

Directions: Take Route K exit off I–55. Turn left on Sprigg, then right onto Broadway.
Phone: (314) 651–3130
Hours: 9:00 A.M.–5:00 P.M., Monday–Friday; 9:00 A.M.–4:00 P.M., Saturday
Credit Cards: MasterCard, Visa
Personal Checks: Yes, with proper identification
Handicapped Accessible: Yes
Food: A variety of restaurants within 6 blocks in downtown area
Bus Tours: Yes

Warehouse of Leathers
261 West Park Mall

Directions: Route K exit off I–55
Phone: (314) 335–3333
Hours: 10:00 A.M.–9:30 P.M., Monday–Saturday; 12:30–5:30 P.M., Sunday, except holidays
Credit Cards: American Express, Discover, Mastercard, Visa
Personal Checks: Yes, with picture driver's license and major credit card
Handicapped Accessible: Yes
Food: Restaurants in the mall
Bus Tours: Yes
Notes or Attractions: Several miles from scenic, French-style waterfront in downtown Cape Girardeau and Trail of Tears State Park

Columbia

Walnut Bowl
Route 2, Box 301

Directions: From I–70 take Millersburg exit MM137. Store is located nine miles east of Columbia.
Phone: (314) 474–7611
Hours: Variable, call ahead
Credit Cards: MasterCard, Visa
Personal Checks: Yes, with identification
Handicapped Accessible: Yes
Food: Available nearby
Bus Tours: Yes

Festus

Florsheim
1159 Gannon Drive

Directions: Take exit 175 from Highway 55
Phone: (314) 933–5153
Hours: 9:00 A.M.–8:00 P.M., Monday–Thursday; 9:00 A.M.–9:00 P.M., Friday; 9:00 A.M.–8:00 P.M., Saturday; noon–5:00 P.M., Sunday
Credit Cards: American Express, Discover, MasterCard, Visa
Personal Checks: Yes, with driver's license identification for out-of-state residents
Handicapped Accessible: Yes
Food: Fast-food available across the street
Bus Tours: Yes

Grandview

Montgomery Ward Clearance Outlet
12344 Highway 71 South

Directions: Blue Ridge Boulevard exit off Highway 71

Phone: (816) 765–4431
Hours: 10:00 A.M.–8:00 P.M., Monday–Friday; 10:00 A.M.–6:00 P.M., Saturday; noon–5:00 P.M., Sunday
Additional Savings: Select merchandise discounted weekly
Credit Cards: American Express, Discover, MasterCard, Montgomery Ward, Visa
Personal Checks: Yes, with driver's license and credit card
Handicapped Accessible: Yes
Food: Restaurants and fast-food on Blue Ridge Boulevard in back of the store
Bus Tours: Yes
Notes or Attractions: Behind Harry S Truman farm home

Shoe Cents
12114 Highway 71 South

Directions: Blue Ridge Boulevard exit off Highway 71 to Truman Corners Shopping Center
Phone: (816) 763–1611
Hours: 10:00 A.M.–9:00 P.M., Monday–Friday; 10:00 A.M.–8:00 P.M., Saturday; noon–5:00 P.M., Sunday
Additional Savings: Seasonal sales in February, March, July, and August
Food: Fast-food nearby
Handicapped Accessible: Yes
Credit Cards: Discover, MasterCard, Visa
Personal Checks: Yes with valid driver's license
Notes or Attractions: Harry S Truman farm home 2 blocks away

Independence

Underwriters Recovery Sales Outlet
13900 E. Thirty-Fifth Street

Directions: I–70 to Noland Road exit north; 7 blocks on Noland Road to Thirty-Fifth Street; left on Thirty-Fifth Street for ½ block. Approximately 15 miles east of downtown Kansas City.
Phone: (816) 252–9666

Hours: 10:00 A.M.–8:00 P.M., Tuesday–Friday; 10:00 A.M.–4:00 P.M., Saturday; noon–6:00 P.M., Sunday
Additional Discounts: Spring and fall sales
Credit Cards: MasterCard, Visa
Personal Checks: Yes, with proper identification
Handicapped Accessible: Yes
Food: Over fifteen food outlets nearby
Bus Tours: Yes
Notes or Attractions: Independence is the hometown of former President Harry S Truman.

Jefferson City

Florsheim
312 Wilson Drive

Directions: Highway 50 to Dix Road north to Industrial Drive west. Travel ¾ mile to Wilson Drive, which is on the left.
Phone: (314) 635–1210
Hours: 10:00 A.M.–5:30 P.M., Monday–Saturday
Credit Cards: American Express, Discover, MasterCard, Visa
Personal Checks: Yes; out-of-state checks require driver's license identification
Handicapped Accessible: Yes
Food: Restaurants and fast-food on Missouri Boulevard, 1 mile away
Bus Tours: Yes
Notes or Attractions: State capitol and governor's mansion in center of Jefferson City, 4 miles away

Jennings

J. C. Penney Outlet Store
Highway 55 at River Road Mall

Directions: Halls Ferry Road at Jennings Station Road
Phone: (314) 868–9700
Hours: 9:00 A.M.–9:00 P.M., Monday–Saturday; 11:00 A.M.–6:00 P.M., Sunday

Credit Cards: American Express, J. C. Penney, MasterCard, Visa
Personal Checks: Yes, with valid driver's license
Handicapped Accessible: Yes
Food: Within 2 miles of the outlet
Bus Tours: Yes
Notes or Attractions: 3 miles outside St. Louis city limits

Joplin

Florsheim
102 Range Line Road

Directions: 3 miles north of exit 8B on I–44. On left side in Mall Plaza.
Phone: (417) 782–8577
Hours: 9:00 A.M.–6:00 P.M., Monday–Saturday; 1:00–5:00 P.M., Sunday
Credit Cards: American Express, Discover, MasterCard, Visa
Personal Checks: Yes; out-of-state checks require driver's license identification
Handicapped Accessible: Yes
Food: Food court in North Park Mall across the street
Bus Tours: Yes, buses can park at North Park Mall

Lebanon

Full Size Fashions
200A Lawson

Directions: Take second Lebanon exit to Highway 5 south; turn right onto Lawson. Outlet located on the corner of Market Street and Lawson Avenue.
Phone: (417) 532–4505
Hours: 9:30 A.M.– 6:30 P.M., Monday–Saturday; closed Sundays
Additional Savings: Seasonal sales held in January and August
Credit Cards: Discover, MasterCard, Visa
Personal Checks: Yes, with driver's license and major credit card
Handicapped Accessible: Yes
Food: Several eateries within 4 blocks
Bus Tours: Yes

Newgate Shirts
200 Lawson Avenue

Directions: Take second Lebanon exit to Highway 5 south; turn right onto Lawson. Outlet located on the corner of Market Street and Lawson Avenue.
Phone: (417) 588–2010
Hours: 9:00 A.M.–6:30 P.M., Monday–Saturday; noon–5:00 P.M., Sunday
Credit Cards: Discover, MasterCard, Visa
Personal Checks: Yes, with proper identification
Handicapped Accessible: Yes
Food: Fast-food stores and restaurants within 4 blocks
Bus Tours: Yes

VF Factory Outlet Mall
2020 Industrial Drive

Directions: I–44 to exit 129 (Highway 5 south); right on Lawson Avenue to Market Street; left into mall
Phone: (417) 588–4142 or (800) 772–VFFO
Hours: January through June 10:00 A.M.–7:00 P.M., Monday–Friday; 9:00 A.M.–7:00 P.M., Saturday; 12:30–5:30 P.M., Sunday. July through December 10:00 A.M.–8:00 P.M., Monday–Friday; 9:00 A.M.–7:00 P.M., Saturday; 12:30–5:30 P.M., Sunday
Additional Savings: End-of-season clearance; Presidents Day and Independence Day sales
Stores:
Banister Shoes
Bass Shoes
Bon Worth
Famous Brands Housewares
Jonathan Logan
Paper Factory
Prestige Fragrance & Cosmetics, Inc.
Reading Bag Company
totes
Van Heusen
VF Factory Outlet

Credit Cards: MasterCard, Visa
Personal Checks: Yes, with picture identification
Handicapped Accessible: Yes
Food: Snack bar at mall, restaurants nearby
Bus Tours: Yes; complimentary coffee and snack for tour leader and bus driver
Notes or Attractions: Trout fishing, camping, and canoeing in Bennett Springs resort area

Walnut Bowl

1078 South Jefferson

Directions: I–44 to exit 129 at Highway 5
Phone: (417) 532–6186
Hours: Vary, call ahead
Credit Cards: MasterCard, Visa
Personal Checks: Yes, with identification
Handicapped Accessible: No
Food: Nearby
Bus Tours: Yes

Osage Beach

Osage Village Factory Merchants, Etc.

Route 54

Directions: Route 54, near Route 42 in the center of Osage Beach
Phone: (314) 348–2065
Hours: March through December 9:00 A.M.–9:00 P.M., Monday–Saturday; 9:00 A.M.–6 P.M., Sunday. January and February 10:00 A.M.–6:00 P.M., daily
Stores:
Aileen
Anne Klein
Banister Shoes
Bass Shoes
Bon Worth
Boston Traders

Bruce Alan Bags
Capezio Shoes
Carter's Childrenswear
Chaus
Corning/Revere
Dansk
Eagle's Eye
Evan Picone/Palm Beach
Factory Shoe Outlet
Gant
GeGe's
Grey Goose
Hanes Activewear
harvé benard
Hathaway
Hensen Lingerie Factory Store
Izod
Jaymar
Jonathan Logan
Jones New York
Kitchen Collection
L'eggs/Hanes/Bali
Lenox
London Fog
Manhattan Factory Store
Nautica
Nike
Olga/Warner
Oneida
OshKosh B'Gosh
Polly Flinders
Prestige Fragrance & Cosmetics, Inc.
Ribbon Outlet, Inc.
Sergio Tacchini
totes/Sunglass World
Toys Unlimited
Van Heusen
Wallet Works

Credit Cards: Most major cards accepted
Handicapped Accessible: Yes
Bus Tours: Ample parking in lot
Notes or Attractions: In the heart of the Missouri Ozarks at Lake of the Ozarks, a family vacation and convention destination

Ozark

Native Wood Products
Highway 14 and Business Highway 65

Directions: At the stop light where Highway 14 and Business Highway 65 intersect
Phone: (417) 485–6683
Hours: 8:00 A.M.–5:00 P.M., Monday–Friday; 9:00 A.M.–5:00 P.M., Saturday, Sunday, and holidays; closed Sundays Thanksgiving through Easter
Credit Cards: Discover, MasterCard, Visa
Personal Checks: Yes, with driver's license
Handicapped Accessible: Yes, except bathrooms at this time
Food: Restaurants and fast food restaurants within 1 mile
Bus Tours: Yes; ample parking
Notes or Attractions: In Ozark Mountain vacation area

Sikeston

Sikeston Factory Outlet Stores
I–55 and Highway 60–62

Directions: At intersection of I–55 and Highway 60–62, ½ mile north of the Highway 57–55 cloverleaf
Phone: (314) 471–2385
Hours: 9:00 A.M.–9:00 P.M., Monday–Saturday; noon–6:00 P.M., Sunday
Stores:
Aileen
Bass Shoes
Black & Decker
Bon Worth

Book Warehouse
Bugle Boy Outlet
Cape Isle Knitters
Carter's Childrenswear
Corning/Revere
Famous Footwear
Florsheim
Fragrance Cove
Full Size Fashions
Geoffrey Beene
Hush Puppies Factory Direct
Izod
Kitchen Collection
Le Creuset
L'eggs/Hanes/Bali
London Fog
Ribbon Outlet, Inc.
S & K Famous Brands
Van Heusen
Wallet Works
Welcome Home
Westport Ltd.

Credit Cards: Most stores accept major credit cards
Personal Checks: Most stores accept personal checks with proper identification
Handicapped Accessible: Yes
Food: Noted local cafe ½ block from the outlet stores
Bus Tours: Yes
Notes or Attractions: Stopping point on the way to Branson, Missouri, with plenty of motels in the area

Wentzville

Belz Factory Outlet Mall
100 Mall Parkway

Directions: Take exit 212A off I–70

Phone: (314) 327–8110
Hours: 10:00 A.M.–9:00 P.M., Monday–Saturday; noon–6:00 P.M., Sunday
Stores:
Aileen
Amy Stoudt
Bag & Baggage
Bookland
Bugle Boy Outlet
Burlington Coat Factory Warehouse
Corning/Revere
Dress Barn
Famous Name Gifts
Farberware
Gitano
Jewelies
Kitchen Collection
L'eggs/Hanes/Bali
Mikasa Factory Store
Old Mill Ladies Sportswear
Old Time Pottery
Paper Factory
Perfumania
Plumm's
Reading Shoe Outlet
Ribbon Outlet, Inc.
Supermarket of Shoes
Top of the Line Cosmetics
Toy Liquidators
Van Heusen
Wegmann's Diamond and Jewelry Mart
WestPoint Pepperell
Credit Cards: Most major cards
Personal Checks: Most merchants accept checks with two forms of identification
Handicapped Accessible: Stores on one level
Food: Food court located in the mall
Bus Tours: Yes

Ohio

Numbers in this legend correspond to the numbers on the accompanying map. The number to the right of each city or town name is the page number on which that municipality's outlets first appear in this book.

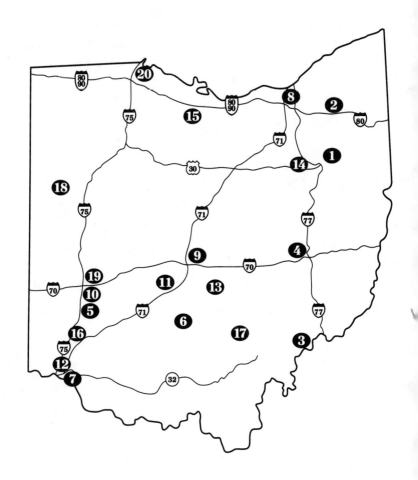

Alliance

Sherwood Coats of Ohio
45 North Arch Street

Directions: In downtown Alliance near routes 62, 183 and 225
Phone: (216) 823–4020
Hours: 10:00 A.M.–4:00 P.M., Monday–Saturday
Additional Savings: Seasonal sales held in January and September
Credit Cards: MasterCard, Visa
Personal Checks: Yes, with driver's license
Handicapped Accessible: Yes
Food: Nearby in downtown area 1½ blocks away
Bus Tours: Yes
Notes or Attractions: Factory tours, if reserved in advance, to groups of ten or more

Aurora

Aurora Farms Factory Outlet
549 S. Chillicothe Road

Directions: Route 43, 1 mile south of Route 82
Phone: (216) 562–2000 or (800) 837–2001
Hours: 10:00 A.M.–6:00 P.M., Monday–Wednesday; 10:00 A.M.–9:00 P.M., Thursday–Saturday; 10:00 A.M.–5:00 P.M., Sunday
Additional Savings: Memorial Day weekend and early August anniversary sidewalk sales
Stores:
Aileen
American Tourister/Buxton
Banister Shoes
Bass Shoes
Cape Isle Knitters
Carlson's Christmas Collection
Carter's Childrenswear
Champion Hanes

Corning/Revere
Crazy Horse
Geoffrey Beene
Gitano
Houseware Outlet
Izod
Jonathan Logan
Jones New York
Leather Loft
L'eggs/Hanes/Bali
Manhattan Factory Store
Paper Factory
Prestige Fragrance & Cosmetics, Inc.
Ribbon Outlet, Inc.
Sequels Book Outlet
Sports Wearhouse
Toy Liquidators
Van Heusen
Wallet Works
Wayside Workshop
Welcome Home
Credit Cards: Most stores accept all major credit cards
Personal Checks: Most stores accept personal checks
Handicapped Accessible: Yes
Food: Restaurant and snack shops on premises
Bus Tours: Yes, coupon brochure featuring additional savings for groups; bus driver and escort receive a $5.00 coin redeemable at stores or eateries
Notes or Attractions: Minutes away from Sea World, Geauga Lake, and Cuyahoga Valley National Recreation Park; year-round flea market and farmers' market held every Wednesday and Sunday

Belpre

Lee Middleton Original Doll Factory Outlet
1301 Washington Boulevard

Directions: I–77 to Route 7 south to Belpre exit (Farson Street going south). From Farson Street turn left onto Washington Boulevard. Factory is in 1½ miles on the right.
Phone: (614) 423–1717 or (800) 843–9572
Hours: 9:00 A.M.–5:00 P.M., Monday–Friday
Additional Savings: 10 percent off the doll of the month
Credit Cards: MasterCard, Visa
Personal Checks: Yes, with identification
Handicapped Accessible: Yes
Food: Drinks, popcorn, and fudge on the premises; restaurants within 1 block
Bus Tours: Yes
Notes or Attractions: Free factory tours by appointment; if wheelchair bound, request factory tour when bus groups aren't scheduled. Near Fenton Art Glass, historic Blennerhasset Island, and Marietta, Ohio, the oldest settlement in the northwest territory.

Cambridge

Boyd's Crystal Art Glass
1203 Morton Avenue

Directions: Exit at Route 209 north from I–70 onto Woodlawn Avenue, then turn left at Morton
Phone: (614) 439–2077
Hours: 8:00 A.M.–4:00 P.M., daily; open Saturday, during June, July, and August, 9:00 A.M.–4:00 P.M.
Additional Savings: Occasional monthly specials
Credit Cards: MasterCard, Visa
Personal Checks: Yes, with identification
Handicapped Accessible: Limited; call ahead for information
Food: Fast-food and sit-down restaurants within 1–5 miles

Bus Tours: Yes; notify prior to visit
Notes or Attractions: Free glass factory tours featuring glass artisans at work

Fostoria Factory Outlet
2311 Southgate Parkway

Directions: From exit 178 off I–70 take Route 209 north to Rax Restaurant; turn right into Deer Creek Motel complex
Phone: (614) 439–3600
Hours: 8:00 A.M.–6:00 P.M., Monday–Sunday
Additional Savings: Seasonal sale usually held in August
Credit Cards: MasterCard, Visa
Personal Checks: Yes, with driver's license
Handicapped Accessible: Yes
Food: Restaurants and fast-food close by
Bus Tours: Yes

Centerville

Hit or Miss
Crosspointe Shopping Center
101 E. Alexandersville–Bellbrook Road

Directions: From I–75 take Route 675 to exit 4A. Turn left from the exit and continue through the first traffic light. Shopping center is on the left.
Phone: (513) 435–4894
Hours: 10:00 A.M.–9:00 P.M., Monday–Saturday; noon–5:00 P.M., Sunday
Additional Savings: Sales during January, February, July, and August
Credit Cards: American Express, Discover, MasterCard, Visa
Personal Checks: Yes, with driver's license
Handicapped Accessible: Yes
Food: In shopping center
Bus Tours: Yes
Notes or Attractions: 30 miles from King's Island Amusement Park and ten minutes from the Air Force Museum

Chillicothe

Kitchen Collection
71 E. Water Street

Directions: From Route 23 take Bridge Street exit (business loop) through shopping district and over the bridge. Turn left at second light onto Water Street. Outlet is 2 blocks farther on the right.
Phone: (614) 773–9150
Hours: 10:00 A.M.–6:00 P.M., Monday–Friday; 10:00 A.M.–5:00 P.M., Saturday; noon–5:00 P.M., Sunday
Additional Savings: Monthly sales
Credit Cards: Discover, MasterCard, Visa
Personal Checks: Yes, with driver's license or photo identification
Handicapped Accessible: Yes
Food: Along Route 23 south business loop
Bus Tours: Yes; 10 percent discount to bus groups
Notes or Attractions: Mound City National Monument 1 mile outside of Chillicothe

Cincinnati

Factory Direct
10737 Reading Road

Directions: From I–75 go north on Reading Road to second light. Outlet is on Route 42.
Phone: (513) 733–0800
Hours: 9:30 A.M.–8:00 P.M., Monday–Friday; 9:00 A.M.–6:00 P.M., Saturday; noon–5:00 P.M., Sunday and holidays
Additional Savings: Special discounts to churches, schools, brides, and volume buyers
Credit Cards: MasterCard, Visa
Personal Checks: Yes, with proper identification
Handicapped Accessible: Yes
Food: Restaurants on the same block
Bus Tours: Yes

Notes or Attractions: 14 miles from downtown Cincinnati and Kings Island, 2 miles from Sharon Woods and 8 miles from Chesterdale Entertainment Center

Hit or Miss

Three Cincinnati locations (call for directions):
11392 Princeton Pike; (513) 671–3081
3960 E. Galbraith Road; (513) 793–3139
7500 Beechmont Mall; (513) 232–5440

Hours: 10:00 A.M.–9:00 P.M., Monday–Saturday; noon–5:00 P.M., Sunday
Credit Cards: American Express, Discover, MasterCard, Visa
Personal Checks: Yes, within a 60-mile radius
Handicapped Accessible: Yes
Food: Fast-food nearby
Bus Tours: Yes

J. C. Penney Outlet Store

8770 Colerain Avenue

Directions: 2 miles south of I–75 on exit 33
Phone: (513) 385–9700
Hours: 10:00 A.M.–9:00 P.M., Monday–Friday; 9:00 A.M.–9:00 P.M., Saturday; 10:00 A.M.–5:30 P.M., Sunday
Additional Savings: Specials advertised weekly
Credit Cards: American Express, MasterCard, J. C. Penney, Visa
Personal Checks: Yes, with proper identification
Handicapped Accessible: Yes
Food: Snack bar in the store
Bus Tours: Yes

Lazarus Final Clearance

2101 E. Kemper Road

Directions: I–275 to Mosteller Road exit; left onto Kemper Road
Phone: (513) 782–1492 (apparel); (513) 782–1477 (electronics); (513) 782–1485 (furniture)

Hours: 10:00 A.M.–9:00 P.M., Monday–Saturday; noon–6:00 P.M., Sunday
Additional Savings: Mark-downs the last Friday of every month
Credit Cards: Lazarus, MasterCard, Visa
Personal Checks: Yes, from residents of Indiana, Kentucky, Ohio, and West Virginia
Handicapped Accessible: Yes
Food: Snack bar area with vending machines and sitting room in the store
Bus Tours: Yes

Outlets Ltd. Mall
I–71 and King Mill Road

Directions: I–71 to exit 25/King Mill Road; outlet is on the left
Phone: (513) 398–5532
Hours: 10:00 A.M.–9:00 P.M., Monday–Saturday; noon–6:00 P.M., Sunday
Stores:
Children's Place
Diamonds Unlimited
Dress Barn
Famous Footwear
Hit or Miss
Paper Factory
Prestige Fragrance & Cosmetics, Inc.
Shoe Manufacturers Outlet
Shoe Sensation
totes
Toy Liquidators
Credit Cards: Most stores accept major credit cards
Personal Checks: Most stores accept checks with two forms of identification
Handicapped Accessible: Yes
Food: Fast-food and restaurants at exit 25
Bus Tours: Yes
Notes or Attractions: Across from King's Island Amusement Park

Polly Flinders

234 E. Eighth Street

Directions: Downtown Cincinnati
Phone: (513) 621–3222
Hours: 9:30 A.M.–5:00 P.M., Monday–Saturday
Credit Cards: MasterCard, Visa
Personal Checks: Yes, with driver's license and major credit card
Handicapped Accessible: No
Food: Restaurants and fast-food in downtown area
Bus Tours: No
Notes or Attractions: Close to all Cincinnati museums and attractions

Shapely Outlet Mall

2430 E. Kemper Road

Directions: I–275 to Mosteller Road exit; left onto Kemper Road; right to mall
Phone: (513) 771–6262
Hours: 10:00 A.M.–9:00 P.M., Monday–Saturday; noon–6:00 P.M., Sunday
Stores:
Annie's Son Shoes
Cotton Mill
Fashion Factory Outlet
Handbag Factory Outlet
Head Factory Store
Jewelies
Newport Sportswear
Old Mill Ladies Sportswear
Paper Warehouse
Polly Flinders
Shapely Factory Outlet
Credit Cards: Stores honor most major credit cards
Personal Checks: Most stores accept checks with two forms of identification
Handicapped Accessible: Yes
Food: Cafe in mall
Bus Tours: Yes

Talbots
Convention Place Mall, Fifth and Elm streets

Directions: In downtown Cincinnati across from the Hyatt Hotel
Phone: (513) 579–0123
Hours: 10:00 A.M.–6:00 P.M., Monday–Saturday
Credit Cards: Most major credit cards accepted
Personal Checks: Yes, with proper identification
Handicapped Accessible: Yes
Food: In mall
Bus Tours: Yes

Whiting Manufacturing Outlet
9999 Carver Road

Directions: From I–71 take the Pfeiffer Road exit, which runs into Reed Hartman Highway. Turn left onto Reed Hartman Highway. Turn onto Carver Road; the Whiting plant is very prominent.
Phone: (513) 791–9100
Hours: 9:00 A.M.–6:00 P.M., Monday–Saturday; 11:00 A.M.–4:00 P.M., Sunday
Credit Cards: Discover, MasterCard, Visa
Personal Checks: Only from Ohio residents
Handicapped Accessible: Yes
Food: Fast-food chains nearby
Bus Tours: Yes

Cleveland

Joseph & Feiss Company Outlet Store
2149 W. Fifty-Third Street

Directions: I–90 to West Forty-Fourth Street exit; turn right onto Clark Avenue, right onto West Fifty-Third Street, and right onto Walworth to rear entrance of outlet
Phone: (216) 961–3907

Hours: 11:00 A.M.–8:00 P.M., Tuesday–Friday; 10:00 A.M.–6:00 P.M., Saturday; 11:00 A.M.–5:00 P.M., Sunday
Additional Savings: Seasonal closeout sales June and December
Credit Cards: MasterCard, Visa
Personal Checks: Yes, with driver's license
Handicapped Accessible: Yes
Food: Fast-food and restaurants within 3 miles
Bus Tours: Yes; call in advance

Columbus

Brice Outlet Mall
Brice and Scarborough roads

Directions: I–70 to Brice Road south exit; go right at first intersection (Scarborough Road); mall is on left
Phone: (614) 863–0884
Hours: 10:00 A.M.–9:00 P.M., Monday–Thursday; 10:00 A.M.–10:00 P.M., Friday and Saturday; noon–6:00 P.M., Sunday
Stores: (Partial listing; not all stores are outlets)
Bon Worth
El-Bee Shoe Outlet
Famous Footware
Handbag Factory Outlet
Ninth Street Bridal and Formal Outlet
Sears Outlet
Shoe Sensation
Watches-N-Stuff
Credit Cards: Most stores accept major credit cards
Personal Checks: Most stores accept checks with two forms of identification
Handicapped Accessible: Yes
Food: In mall
Bus Tours: Yes
Notes or Attractions: Near Brice Road Consumer Square shopping center and J. C. Penney Outlet. Super Saver Cinemas, with eight screens and $1.50 admission at all times, is in mall.

Burlington Coat Factory Warehouse
270 Graceland Boulevard

Directions: I–71 to Morse Road exit; west on Morse to Route 23 (High Street) intersection. Turn right onto High. At first light turn left onto Graceland Boulevard, which takes you into the shopping center.
Phone: (614) 885–2628
Hours: 10:00 A.M.–9:00 P.M., Monday–Saturday; 11:00 A.M.–6:00 P.M., Sunday
Credit Cards: American Express, Discover, MasterCard, Visa
Personal Checks: Yes, with driver's license
Handicapped Accessible: Yes
Food: Fast-food nearby
Bus Tours: Yes

Dress Barn/Dress Barn Woman
Six Columbus locations (call for directions):
7624 New Market Center Way; (614) 764–0557
7632 New Market Center Way; (614) 791–8030
7656 New Market Center Way; (614) 889–7990
5610 Cleveland Avenue; (614) 882–5533
6464 Tussing Road; (614) 863–0041
759 Bethel Road; (614) 538–0538

Hours: 10:00 A.M.–9:00 P.M., Monday–Saturday; noon–5:00 P.M., Sunday
Food: Fast-food nearby
Handicapped Accessible: Yes
Credit Cards: American Express, Discover, MasterCard, Visa
Personal Checks: Yes, with driver's license and major credit card
Bus Tours: Yes

Hit or Miss
Six Columbus locations (call for directions):
2025 W. Henderson Road; (614) 451–0628
2707 Northland Plaza Drive; (614) 523–1786
3872 E. Broad Street; (614) 237–8090
4428 Crossroad Center; (614) 864–3967

121 S. High Street; (614) 461–0550
New Market Center Way (see listing under NewMarket Mall)

Hours: 10:00 A.M.–9:00 P.M., Monday–Saturday; noon–5:00 P.M., Sunday
Additional Savings: Merchandise marked down frequently
Credit Cards: American Express, Discover, MasterCard, Visa
Personal Checks: Yes, within 60-mile radius
Handicapped Accessible: Yes
Food: Fast-food nearby; stores located in shopping districts
Bus Tours: Yes

J. C. Penney Outlet Store
Brice Road

Directions: I–70 to Brice Road south. Turn right at first light onto Scarborough Road. Building is 1 mile on left.
Phone: (614) 868–0250
Hours: 9:00 A.M.–9:00 P.M., Monday–Saturday; 10:00 A.M.–7:00 P.M., Sunday
Additional Savings: Weekly advertised sales plus seasonal clearance sales
Credit Cards: American Express, J. C. Penney, MasterCard, Visa
Personal Checks: Yes, with driver's license and major credit card
Handicapped Accessible: Yes
Food: Snack bar in store; fast-food and restaurants at Brice and Scarborough roads
Bus Tours: Yes
Notes or Attractions: Close to all Columbus events and attractions

Lazarus Final Clearance
141 S. High Street

Directions: Intersection of S. High and W. Town streets in center city; store at Front Street level
Phone: (614) 463–3520
Hours: 10:00 A.M.–9:00 P.M., Monday–Friday; 10:00 A.M.–6:00 P.M., Saturday; noon–6:00 P.M., Sunday
Additional Savings: Mark-downs the last Friday of every month

Credit Cards: Lazarus, MasterCard, Visa
Personal Checks: Yes, two identifications required; one must include a picture
Handicapped Accessible: Yes
Food: Fast-food and restaurants in downtown area; links into City Center Mall food court
Bus Tours: Yes

NewMarket Mall
7581 New Market Center Way

Directions: Take exit 20 (Sawmill Road) off I–270 and head north; mall entrance is on the right
Phone: (614) 766–6777
Hours: 10:00 A.M.–9:00 P.M., Monday–Saturday; noon–6:00 P.M., Sunday
Additional Savings: Seasonal sales the third weekend in January, the second weekend in March, and the second weekend in July
Stores: (Partial listing; not all stores are outlets)
Capers
Casual Male Big and Tall
Dress Barn/Dress Barn Woman
El-Bee Shoe Outlet
Famous Footwear
Finish Line
Hit or Miss
Kitchen Place
Linens 'n Things
Old Mill Ladies Sportswear
S & K Famous Brands
Shoe Sensation
Credit Cards: Stores accept most major credit cards
Personal Checks: Most stores require two forms of identification
Handicapped Accessible: Yes
Food: Food court in the mall
Bus Tours: Yes
Notes or Attractions: Near Columbus Zoo and historic Old Dublin; other Columbus attractions one-half hour away

Nu-Look Fashions Outlet Store

5080 Sinclair Road

Directions: I–71 to Morse Road west exit; turn right onto Sinclair Road; store on right side
Phone: (614) 885–4936
Hours: 10:00 A.M.–7:00 P.M., Monday–Friday; 10:00 A.M.–6:00 P.M., Saturday
Credit Cards: MasterCard, Visa
Personal Checks: Yes, with driver's license
Handicapped Accessible: One step into store; security guard or store personnel will provide assistance
Food: Fast-food and restaurants all along Morse Road
Bus Tours: Yes

Pepperidge Farm

1174 Kenny Center

Directions: Call ahead
Phone: (614) 457–4800
Hours: 10:00 A.M.–6:00 P.M., Monday–Friday; 10:00 A.M.–5:00 P.M., Saturday
Additional Savings: In-store specials every week
Credit Cards: Cash only
Personal Checks: Cash only
Handicapped Accessible: Yes
Food: Fast-food and restaurants along Kenny Road
Bus Tours: Yes

Sears Outlet

Two Columbus locations (call for directions):
4545 Fisher Road; (614) 272–3001
Brice Outlet Mall; (614) 863–0884

Hours: 10:00 A.M.–9:00 P.M., Monday–Friday; 10:00 A.M.–6:00 P.M., Saturday; noon–5:00 P.M., Sunday
Credit Cards: Discover, Sears

Personal Checks: Yes, with driver's license and major credit card
Handicapped Accessible: Yes
Food: Fast-food in mall or nearby
Bus Tours: Yes

Sycamore
2625 Northland Plaza Drive

Directions: I–71 to Morse Road exit; turn right. Northland Mall is on right side about 1 mile from exit.
Phone: (614) 891–9303
Hours: 10:00 A.M.–9:00 P.M., Monday–Saturday; noon–5:00 P.M., Sunday
Credit Cards: Discover, MasterCard, Visa
Personal Checks: Yes, with driver's license
Handicapped Accessible: Yes
Food: In mall
Bus Tours: Yes

Dayton

Book Warehouse
Corners at the Mall Shopping Center
231 Springboro Pike

Directions: Call ahead
Phone: (513) 438–9119
Hours: 10:00 A.M.–9:00 P.M., Monday–Saturday; noon–5:00 P.M., Sunday
Credit Cards: Diners Club, Discover, MasterCard, Visa
Personal Checks: Yes
Handicapped Accessible: Yes, with handicapped parking in front of store
Food: Fast-food and restaurants in front of shopping center
Bus Tours: Yes
Notes or Attractions: Air Force Museum, the oldest and largest military aviation museum in the world, is located at Wright–Patterson Air Force Base; a self-guided Aviation Trail, connecting historic aviation sites, is also in Dayton

Hit or Miss

Salem Mall, 5200 Salem Avenue

Directions: Call ahead
Phone: (513) 837–2817
Hours: 10:00 A.M.–9:00 P.M., Monday–Saturday; noon–5:00 P.M., Sunday
Additional Savings: Merchandise marked down frequently
Credit Cards: American Express, Discover, MasterCard, Visa
Personal Checks: Yes, within a 60-mile radius
Handicapped Accessible: Yes
Food: Available in and near shopping center
Bus Tours: Yes
Notes or Attractions: See notes under Book Warehouse, Dayton

Midwest Glass & China Outlet

6425 N. Dixie Drive

Directions: From I–75 take exit 58 west (Needmore Road) ½ mile to N. Dixie Drive; store is located ½ mile north on west side of N. Dixie Drive
Phone: (513) 890–1009
Hours: 10:00 A.M.–6:00 P.M., Monday–Saturday; noon–4:00 P.M., Sunday in November and December
Credit Cards: MasterCard, Visa
Personal Checks: Yes, with identification
Handicapped Accessible: Yes, with entrance ramp, wide aisles, and first floor rest room
Food: Restaurant next door
Bus Tours: Yes
Notes or Attractions: See notes under Book Warehouse, Dayton

Jeffersonville

At press time, two outlet malls along Route 71 in the Jeffersonville area are in the final stages of completion. For more information, call the Ohio division of Tourism at 1–800–BUCKEYE.

Lakeland

totes
10078 E. Kemper Road

Directions: Take Loveland/Indian Hill exit 52 off I–275. At end of exit turn left. Turn right at E. Kemper Road; store is ½ mile on the left.
Phone: (513) 583–2390
Hours: 10:00 A.M.–6:00 P.M., Monday–Friday; 9:00 A.M.–5:00 P.M., Saturday; noon–5:00 P.M., Sunday
Credit Cards: Discover, MasterCard, Visa
Personal Checks: Yes, with proper identification
Handicapped Accessible: Not accessible, but staff will assist someone in a wheelchair
Food: Fast-food and restaurants ½ mile away in Loveland
Bus Tours: Yes
Notes or Attractions: Castle LaRusch nearby, on the banks of the Miami River

Lancaster

Footsaver Shoe Outlet
1273 North Memorial Drive

Directions: On Route 33 at Plaza Shopping Center
Phone: (614) 687–3322
Hours: 10:00 A.M.–5:00 P.M., Monday–Saturday
Additional Savings: Seasonal sales every three to four months
Credit Cards: Discover, MasterCard, Visa
Personal Checks: Yes, with driver's license or picture identification
Handicapped Accessible: Yes
Food: Fast-food, diners, and restaurants along Route 33
Bus Tours: Yes
Notes or Attractions: Close to Wahkeena and Schallenbarger nature preserves. More than ten covered bridges within a 15-mile radius.

Kitchen Collection
621 N. Memorial Drive

Directions: On Route 33 at the intersection of Sixth Avenue and Memorial Drive
Phone: (614) 687–1750
Hours: January and February 9:00 A.M.–6:00 P.M., Monday–Saturday; noon–6:00 P.M., Sunday. March through December 9:00 A.M.–8:00 P.M., Monday–Saturday; noon–6:00 P.M., Sunday.
Additional Savings: Monthly sales
Credit Cards: Discover, MasterCard, Visa
Personal Checks: Yes, with driver's license or photo identification
Handicapped Accessible: Yes
Food: Along Route 33
Bus Tours: Yes; 10 percent discount to bus groups

Massillon

Ekco Housewares
359 State Avenue, NW

Directions: Take Route 77 to 172 west (Lincoln Way); turn right onto Erie and left onto Cherry; cross over Route 21 and a bridge; turn right immediately after bridge onto Third Street. Signs are posted for remainder of route.
Phone: (216) 832–5026
Hours: 10:30 A.M.–2:00 P.M., Tuesday and Thursday
Credit Cards: No
Personal Checks: Yes, with driver's license
Handicapped Accessible: No
Food: Fast-food within 1 mile
Bus Tours: No
Notes or Attractions: Small parking lot for customers

Milan

Lake Erie Factory Outlet
11001 Route 250 North

Directions: On Route 250, ½ mile north of exit 7 on the Ohio Turnpike (I–80/90) and 5 miles south of Route 2
Phone: (419) 499–2528 or (800) 344–5221
Hours: January through March 10:00 A.M.–6:00 P.M., Monday–Thursday; 10:00 A.M.–9:00 P.M., Friday–Saturday; noon–6:00 P.M., Sunday. April through December 10:00 A.M.–9:00 P.M., Monday–Saturday, 10:00 A.M.–6:00 P.M., Sunday
Additional Savings: Sidewalk sales in April, July, September, and October
Stores:
Aileen
American Tourister/Buxton
Arrow Factory Store
Banister Shoes
Bass Shoes
Brass Factory Outlet
Bugle Boy Outlet
Champion Hanes
China Plus
Corning/Revere
Factory Linens
Famous Footwear
Famous Brands Housewares
Farberware
Gitano
Izod
Judy Bond
Kelli's
Kitchen Collection
Leather Loft
L'eggs/Hanes/Bali
Mikasa Factory Store
No Nonsense

Old Mill Ladies Sportswear
Olga/Warner
Paper Factory
Prestige Fragrance & Cosmetics, Inc.
Ruff Hewn
S & K Famous Brands
Socks Galore
Swank
Sweatshirt Company
Toy Liquidators
Van Heusen
Wallet Works
Welcome Home
Wemco Factory Store
Westport Ltd.
What On Earth
Credit Cards: Most major credit cards accepted
Personal Checks: Most stores accept personal checks with two forms of identification
Handicapped Accessible: Yes
Food: Food court in mall
Bus Tours: Yes
Notes or Attractions: Reserved parking for buses, recreational vehicles, and campers. Located near Lake Erie beaches and resorts, wineries, and Cedar Point Amusement Park

Monroe

Fostoria Factory Outlet
1009 Lebanon Street

Directions: I–71 to Lebanon exit/Route 63; turn right and continue until Route 63 intersects with I–75
Phone: (513) 539–9632
Hours: 8:00 A.M.–6:00 P.M., Monday–Sunday
Additional Sales: Seasonal sale usually held in August
Credit Cards: MasterCard, Visa

Personal Checks: Yes, with driver's license
Handicapped Accessible: Yes
Food: Next door
Bus Tours: Yes

Nelsonville

Rocky Boot Outlet
State Road 33

Directions: Brick factory building located at the intersection of Route 33 and Hocking Street; factory outlet in back
Phone: (614) 753–3130
Hours: 9:00 A.M.–7:00 P.M., Monday–Saturday; 11:30 A.M.–5:30 P.M., Sunday
Credit Cards: Discover, MasterCard, Visa
Personal Checks: Yes, with driver's license
Handicapped Accessible: On notification, personnel will assist in bringing customer through factory
Food: Fast-food and restaurants along Route 33
Bus Tours: Yes
Notes or Attractions: Near Hocking Valley Scenic Railroad

St. Marys

Cotton Mill Store
119 E. High Street

Directions: From I–75 take Route 33 west to Route 66; continue on Route 66 to the St. Marys exit; make a right onto High Street, then left into store
Phone: (419) 394–3064
Hours: 9:30 A.M.–8:00 P.M., Monday; 9:30 A.M.–5:00 P.M., Tuesday–Thursday and Saturday; 9:30 A.M.–9:00 P.M., Friday; noon–5:00 P.M., Sunday
Additional Savings: Holiday clearance first two weeks in January; spring clearance for two weeks from first Thursday in March; summer clearance for two weeks from first Thursday in August

Credit Cards: Discover, MasterCard, Visa
Personal Checks: Yes, with name printed on check, driver's license, and major credit card
Handicapped Accessible: Yes, with ramp and railing
Food: In downtown St. Marys, several minutes' walk away
Bus Tours: Yes
Notes or Attractions: Near St. Marys Lake and Erie Canal

Tipp City

Trophy Nut Store
320 N. Second Street

Directions: From I–75 take exit 68/State Route 571 east; cross railroad tracks; third traffic light after tracks is Second Street; turn left to plant and store
Phone: (513) 667–8478
Hours: 9:00 A.M.–5:00 P.M., Monday–Friday; 9:00 A.M.–2:00 P.M., Saturday
Additional Savings: During fall and Christmas seasons
Credit Cards: Yes
Personal Checks: Yes
Handicapped Accessible: Call ahead; they will bring you through the back door to avoid steps
Food: Within 3 blocks
Bus Tours: Yes

Toledo

Haas-Jordan Company
1447 Summit Street

Directions: From I–280 take Summit Street exit toward downtown. Go 1 block west on Summit Street; outlet is on the right side.
Phone: (419) 243–2189
Hours: 9:00 A.M.–4:00 P.M., Monday–Friday
Credit Cards: MasterCard, Visa
Personal Checks: No

Handicapped Accessible: No
Food: Restaurants within 1 mile
Bus Tours: No
Notes or Attractions: Less than 1 mile from downtown Toledo, the Libbey Glass Factory Outlet, and Tony Packo's Cafe, made famous by the television series "M*A*S*H"

Libbey Glass Factory Outlet
1205 Buckeye Street

Directions: From I–280 turn right at the Manhattan exit; then make a quick left onto Buckeye Street, adjacent to the glass factory.
Phone: (419) 727–2374
Hours: June through December 9:30 A.M.–5:30 P.M., Monday–Saturday; noon–5:00 P.M., Sunday
Credit Cards: MasterCard, Visa
Personal Checks: Yes, with identification
Handicapped Accessible: Yes
Food: Within 1 mile
Bus Tours: Yes; $5.00 gift certificate given to driver and tour guide
Notes or Attractions: Near Lake Erie

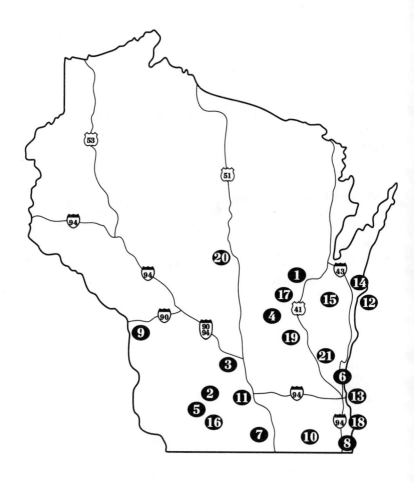

Wisconsin

Numbers in this legend correspond to the numbers on the accompanying map. The number to the right of each city or town name is the page number on which that municipality's outlets first appear in this book.

Appleton

Benetton
Fox River Mall
4301 W. Wisconsin Avenue

Directions: From Highway 41 take Highway 10 exit
Phone: (414) 734–0773
Hours: 10:00 A.M.–9:00 P.M., Monday–Friday; 10:00 A.M.–6:00 P.M., Saturday; 11:00 A.M.–5:00 P.M., Sunday
Additional Savings: February and August
Credit Cards: American Express, MasterCard, Visa
Personal Checks: Yes, with identification
Handicapped Accessible: Yes
Food: Food court in mall
Bus Tours: Yes
Notes or Attractions: 15 miles from EAA Air Adventure Museum in Oshkosh, 35 miles from Green Bay Packer Hall of Fame

Burlington Coat Factory Warehouse
641 Westhill Boulevard

Directions: Located in Westhill Plaza, east of Highway 41 and across from Fox River Mall
Phone: (414) 749–2100 or (800) 444–2628
Hours: 10:00 A.M.–9:30 P.M., Monday–Saturday; 11:00 A.M.–6:00 P.M., Sunday
Credit Cards: American Express, Discover, MasterCard, Visa
Personal Checks: Yes, with proper identification
Handicapped Accessible: Yes
Food: Across the street in Fox River Mall
Bus Tours: Yes

Presto Products Factory Outlet
1831 W. Winnebago Street

Directions: 2 blocks west of Appleton West High School

Phone: (414) 738–1440
Hours: 9:00 A.M.–4:50 P.M., Monday–Friday
Additional Savings: 5 percent discounts for sales over $500 and to non-profit organizations. Monthly specials when select merchandise is marked down 20 to 25 percent below wholesale.
Credit Cards: None
Personal Checks: Yes, with driver's license
Handicapped Accessible: Yes
Food: 2 blocks away
Bus Tours: Yes

Arena

AMPI Morning Glory Farms
Box 127, Highway 14

Directions: 30 miles west of Madison and 8 miles east of Spring Green on Highway 14
Phone: (608) 753–2501
Hours: 8:30 A.M.–7:00 P.M., daily
Additional Savings: In-store specials
Credit Cards: MasterCard, Visa
Personal Checks: Yes, with driver's license
Handicapped Accessible: Yes
Food: Available at store
Bus Tours: Yes
Notes or Attractions: Observation window enables visitors to view the manufacturing process

Baraboo

Flambeau Outlet Store
611 Hitchcock Street

Directions: Corner of South Bend and Hitchcock Street, also known as City 12
Phone: (608) 356–3602

Hours: 10:00 A.M.–5:00 P.M., Tuesday–Saturday
Additional Savings: Occasional
Credit Cards: None
Personal Checks: Yes, with identification
Handicapped Accessible: Yes
Food: Restaurants within 2 blocks
Bus Tours: Yes
Notes or Attractions: Home of the Circus World Museum

Berlin

Midwestern Sport Togs Outlet
150 W. Franklin

Directions: In downtown Berlin, 20 miles west of Oshkosh on Route 116 at intersection with Route 49
Hours: 8:00 A.M.–5:00 P.M., Monday–Friday; 8:00 A.M.–noon, Saturdays from May to Labor Day; 8:00 A.M.–5:00 P.M., Saturdays from Labor Day to April; 10:00 A.M.–3:00 P.M., Sundays Thanksgiving through Christmas
Additional Savings: Fur and leather one-day sale last weekend in August
Credit Cards: MasterCard, Visa
Personal Checks: Yes, with driver's license
Handicapped Accessible: Yes
Food: Within 2 blocks
Bus Tours: Yes
Notes or Attractions: Plant tours available with advance notice

Dodgeville

Lands' End Outlet Store
113 N. Iowa Street

Directions: Highway 151 to Highway 23/Bequette Street; outlet is on the right at the intersection of Bequette and Iowa streets
Phone: (608) 935–9053
Hours: 9:00 A.M.–6:00 P.M., Monday–Thursday; 9:00 A.M.–8:00 P.M., Fri-

day; 9:00 A.M.–5:00 P.M., Saturday; 11:00 A.M.–4:00 P.M., Sunday
Credit Cards: American Express, MasterCard, Visa
Personal Checks: Yes, with proper identification
Handicapped Accessible: Yes
Food: Within 2 miles
Bus Tours: Yes

Fox Point

Country Club Outlet
Brown Port Shopping Center, 8777 N. Port Washington Road

Directions: I–43 to Brown Deer Road exit; Brown Port Shopping Center is immediately on the right
Phone: (414) 352–1215
Hours: 10:00 A.M.–6:00 P.M., Monday–Friday; 10:00 A.M.–5:00 P.M., Saturday; 11:00 A.M.–4:00 P.M., Sunday
Credit Cards: MasterCard, Visa
Personal Checks: Yes, with proper identification
Handicapped Accessible: Yes
Food: Fast food next door
Bus Tours: Yes

Janesville

Monterey Mills Outlet
1725 E. Delavan Drive

Directions: From I–90 take exit 175A (Janesville/Delavan); go right on County Road J and then right at the next intersection onto County Road O, which is Delavan Drive. Outlet is 1 mile further on right side.
Phone: (608) 754–8309, (800) 438–6387
Hours: 8:00 A.M.–4:30 P.M., Monday–Friday; 8:00 A.M.–noon, Saturday
Credit Cards: MasterCard, Visa
Personal Checks: Yes, with driver's license and phone number noted on check
Handicapped Accessible: New handicapped-accessible store should be

open by September 1993
Food: Restaurants 2–3 miles from outlet
Bus Tours: Yes, but must notify first
Notes or Attractions: Near General Motors plant and historic Tallman House

Kenosha

Factory Outlet Center
7700 120th Avenue

Directions: I–94 to Kenosha/Lake Geneva exit 344. Take Route 50 going west; outlet center is on left.
Phone: (414) 857–7961
Hours: January through June 9:30 A.M.–9:00 P.M., Monday–Friday; 9:30 A.M.–6:00 P.M., Saturday; 11:00 A.M.–5:00 P.M., Sunday. July through December 9:30 A.M.–9:00 P.M., Monday–Friday; 9:30 A.M.–8:00 P.M., Saturday; 10:00 A.M.–6:00 P.M., Sunday
Stores:
Aileen
Ambrosia Chocolate & Cocoa
American Tourister/Buxton
Athletic Shoe Factory
Aunt Mary's Yarns
Banister Shoes
Barbizon
Bon Worth
Bootery Outlet
The Brighter Side
Bristol County
Brownberry Bakery Outlet
C.S.O.
Carole Hochman Lingerie
Carter's Childrenswear
Casual Male Big and Tall
Chicago Records
Clothes Outs

Clothing by Farah
The Company Store
The Cookie Jar Cookie Outlet
Corning/Revere
Create-a-Book
Dicken's Books
Dress Barn
Eddie Bauer
Farberware
Fieldcrest Cannon
Frugal Frank's
Fuller Brush
Fureal Leathers
Gentlemen's Wear House
Gift Outlet
Gitano
Great Midwest Craftmarket
Hanes Activewear
Helly-Hansen
Hit or Miss
Home Decor Outlet
Houseware Outlet
Izod
Jonathan Logan
Julie's Jewelry
Just My Size
Kids Ca'pers
Kids Express
Knits by K.T.
LaCrosse Footwear, Inc.
L'eggs/Hanes/Bali
Lehmann's Danish Bakery and Kringle Outlet
Little Red Shoe House
Loomcraft Home Decorating Fabrics
Manhattan Factory Store
Maternity Wearhouse
Mid America Shoe Factory Outlet
Mill City Outlet

Mitchell Leather Shop
Multiples
Newport Sportswear
New Visions
Paint and Wallpaper Factory Outlet
Paper Factory
Perfume Boutique
Rainbow Fashions
Regal Ware Outlet
Ribbon Outlet, Inc.
S & K Famous Brands
Socks Galore and More
Sony Factory Outlet Center
Sweatshirt Company
Top of the Line Cosmetics
totes
Toy Liquidators
Van Heusen
Wallet Works
Welcome Home
West Bend Company Store
Whitewater Gloves
Winona Knits
World Bazaar
Credit Cards: Most stores accept American Express, Discover, Master-Card, Visa
Personal Checks: Most stores accept checks with two forms of identification
Handicapped Accessible: Yes
Food: Food court with over ten eateries to please everyone's taste
Bus Tours: Yes

Lakeside Marketplace Outlet Center
11211 120th Avenue

Directions: I–94 to exit 347, 3 miles from Highway 50
Phone: (414) 857–2101

Hours: 9:00 A.M.–9:00 P.M., Monday–Saturday; 11:00 A.M.–7:00 P.M., Sunday
Stores:
Adolfo II
American Tourister/Buxton
Anko Also
Anne Klein
Bass Shoes
Benetton
Boston Trader Kids
Boston Traders
Brands
Brass Factory Outlet
Calvin Klein
Cambridge Dry Goods
Cape Isle Knitters
Capezio Shoes
Carroll Reed
Chaus
Crazy Horse
Diane Gilman
E. J. Plum
Etienne Aigner
Evan Picone
Famous Brands Housewares
Fanny Farmer
Fila
Galt Sand
Generra
Geoffrey Beene
Gitano
Great Outdoor Clothing
harvé benard
Hensen Lingerie Factory Store
I. B. Diffusion
Jaymar
J. Crew
JH Collectibles
Joan & David

John Henry & Friends
Jones New York
Jordache
Just Kids Outlet Store
Kenneth Cole Shoes
Kitchen Collection
Kristina K. Outlet
Leather Loft
Leslie Fay
Liz Claiborne
Madeleine Fashions
Magnavox
Maidenform
Mikasa Factory Store
Napier Jewelery
Naturalizer
Nike
North Face
OshKosh B'Gosh
Perfumania
Prestige Fragrance & Cosmetics, Inc.
Publishers Outlet
Ruff Hewn
Sassafras
Stone Mountain Handbags
Tanner
Toys Unlimited
Van Heusen
Wemco Factory Store
Woolrich
Zubaz

Credit Cards: Most stores honor most major credit cards
Personal Checks: Most stores accept checks with two forms of identification
Handicapped Accessible: Yes
Food: Restaurant in mall plus vending machines in lounge
Notes or Attractions: Near Lake Michigan, approximately 47 miles from Chicago and 35 miles from Milwaukee

LaCrosse

LaCrosse Footwear Factory Outlet
1320 Saint Andrew Street

Directions: Take exit 3 off I–90 to Route 35 south; turn left onto Saint Andrew Street to outlet
Phone: (608) 782–5630
Hours: Call ahead
Additional Savings: Five-day tent sale in late September or early October
Credit Cards: Discover, MasterCard, Visa
Personal Checks: Yes, with driver's license
Handicapped Accessible: Yes
Food: Around the corner on Lang Drive
Bus Tours: Yes
Notes or Attractions: Close to cruises on the Mississippi River and to the Myrick Park Zoo

Lake Geneva

Country Club Outlet
Fancy Fair Mall, 830 Main Street

Directions: From I–94 take Lake Geneva exit onto Highway 50. Mall located ½ block west of Highway 50 and Broad Street
Phone: (414) 248–9620
Hours: 10:00 A.M.–5:30 P.M., Monday–Saturday; 11:00 A.M.,–5:00 P.M., Sunday
Additional Savings: During Maxwell Street Days in August
Credit Cards: MasterCard, Visa
Personal Checks: Yes, with proper identification
Handicapped Accessible: Yes
Food: Restaurants ½ block away; fast-food 1 mile away
Bus Tours: Yes
Notes or Attractions: Lake Geneva summer resort community

Madison

Lands' End Outlet/Not Quite Perfect stores
411 S. State Street

Directions: Near Lake Mendota, on State Street between West Gilman and West Gorham, close to capitol
Phone: (608) 257–4900
Hours: 10:00 A.M.–8:00 P.M., Monday and Thursday; 10:00 A.M.–6:00 P.M., Tuesday, Wednesday, Friday, and Saturday; 11:00 A.M.–5:00 P.M., Sunday
Credit Cards: American Express, MasterCard, Visa
Personal Checks: Yes, with driver's license and major credit card
Handicapped Accessible: Yes, but aisles are narrow; will move racks to accommodate wheelchairs
Food: Several restaurants within 2 blocks
Bus Tours: Yes

Lands' End Outlet Store
West Towne Shopping Center, 6743 Odana Road

Directions: From West Beltline Highway (routes 12 and 14) exit onto Gammon Road. Turn right onto Odana Road. Outlet is on the right.
Phone: (608) 833–3343
Hours: 9:00 A.M.–9:00 P.M., Monday–Friday; 9:00 A.M.–6:00 P.M., Saturday; 11:00 A.M.–5:00 P.M., Sunday
Credit Cards: American Express, MasterCard, Visa
Personal Checks: Yes, with driver's license and major credit card
Handicapped Accessible: Yes
Food: In or near shopping center
Bus Tours: Yes

Manitowoc

Schuette Factory Outlet
814 Jay Street

Directions: On Jay Street between South Eighth and South Ninth streets
Phone: (414) 684–5521 extension 25 or (800) 558–7740 extension 2777
Hours: 9:00 A.M.–8:00 P.M., Monday–Friday; 9:00 A.M.–5:00 P.M., Saturday; noon–5:00 P.M., Sunday
Additional Savings: Special sales in April and October; Dollar Days monthly
Credit Cards: MasterCard, Visa
Personal Checks: Yes; out-of-state checks need driver's license and identification
Handicapped Accessible: Yes
Food: Restaurants within walking distance
Bus Tours: Yes

Milwaukee

Everitt Knitting Mill Outlet Store
234 W. Florida Street

Directions: Take National Avenue exit from I–94; go 4 blocks north on National Avenue to Florida Street between Second and Third streets south of downtown
Phone: (414) 276–4647
Hours: 10:00 A.M.–4:00 P.M., Monday–Friday
Credit Cards: None
Personal Checks: Yes; Wisconsin only
Handicapped Accessible: No
Food: Snack shops 2–3 blocks away, top restaurants in downtown Milwaukee
Bus Tours: Yes

Lands' End Outlet/Combo stores

6780 W. Brown Deer Rd.

Directions: Route 181 north to Seventy-Sixth Street; go right on West Brown Deer Road; store on left side across the street from Sixty-Eighth Street

Phone: (414) 362–6940

Hours: 10:00 A.M.–9:00 P.M., Monday–Friday; 10:00 A.M.–6:00 P.M., Saturday; 11:00 A.M.–5:00 P.M., Sunday

Credit Cards: American Express, MasterCard, Visa

Personal Checks: Yes, with driver's license and major credit card

Handicapped Accessible: Yes

Food: 4 blocks from restaurants in North Ridge shopping area and mall

Bus Tours: Yes

Mitchell Leather Factory Store

226 N. Water Street

Directions: From I–94 take Route 794 east to Plankinton Avenue exit. Go across the bridge and turn left on Water Street. Outlet is 1½ blocks farther on N. Water Street.

Phone: (414) 272–5942

Hours: 10:00 A.M.–4:30 P.M., Monday–Saturday

Additional Savings: Specials of the week slash an additional 10 to 20 percent off already discounted prices

Credit Cards: MasterCard, Visa

Personal Checks: Yes, with driver's license

Handicapped Accessible: No

Food: Restaurants 1 block away

Bus Tours: Call for arrangements

Purdy Products

1526 N. Thirty-First Street

Directions: Expressway to Thirty-Fifth Street exit; north on Thirty-Fifth to Uliet; east on Uliet to Thirty-First Street; continue north 2 blocks

Phone: (414) 342–5733
Hours: 8:00 A.M.–4:00 P.M., Monday–Friday
Credit Cards: MasterCard, Visa
Personal Checks: Yes, with proper identification
Handicapped Accessible: Yes
Food: 5 blocks away
Bus Tours: Yes

Mishicot

Andercraft Woods
Route 1, Box 91

Directions: Highway 147 to Mishicot; east on Church Street to Andercraft, located on south side of street
Phone: (414) 755–4014
Hours: 8:00 A.M.–4:30 P.M., Monday–Friday; 9:00 A.M.–4:00 P.M., Saturday; 1:00–4:00 P.M., Sunday
Credit Cards: MasterCard, Visa
Personal Checks: Yes, with identification
Handicapped Accessible: Yes
Food: Restaurants ½ mile from factory
Bus Tours: Yes

Neenah

Jersild Factory Store
318 First Street

Directions: Take Main Street exit from Highway 41. Follow signs for hospital; store is 1 block north of Theda Clark Hospital
Phone: (414) 725–6912
Hours: 9:00 A.M.–5:00 P.M., Monday–Friday; 9:00 A.M.–4:00 P.M., Saturday
Credit Cards: MasterCard, Visa
Personal Checks: Yes, with driver's license
Handicapped Accessible: Yes
Food: Convenience store across the street

Bus Tours: Yes
Notes or Attractions: Factory tours, lasting thirty to forty minutes, are available for groups of ten or more; reservations necessary

New Glarus

Swiss Miss
Highway 69 south at Eleventh Avenue

Directions: One-half hour south of Madison on Highway 69
Phone: (608) 527–2514
Hours: 9:00 A.M.–5:00 P.M., Monday–Saturday; noon–4:00 P.M., Sunday
Additional Savings: Additional 10 percent discount Thanksgiving through Christmas
Credit Cards: None
Personal Checks: Yes, with identification
Handicapped Accessible: Yes
Food: Across the street
Bus Tours: Yes
Notes or Attractions: Free factory tours Monday–Friday, 8:00 A.M.–4:00 P.M.

Oshkosh

Carolina Designs Factory Outlet
627 Bay Shore Drive

Directions: 5 blocks off Main Street on Lake Winnebago
Phone: (414) 231–9620
Hours: 10:00 A.M.–5:00 P.M., Monday–Saturday
Additional Savings: Summer sale last week in July to third week in August; Christmas sale after Thanksgiving to December 24
Credit Cards: American Express, Discover, MasterCard, Visa
Personal Checks: Yes, with two forms of identification
Handicapped Accessible: Yes
Food: Restaurants within several blocks
Bus Tours: Yes

Notes or Attractions: On Lake Winnebago and near EAA Air Adventure Museum

Manufacturers Marketplace
3001 S. Washburn

Directions: On Route 41 south of Highway 44
Phone: (414) 231–8911
Hours: 10:00 A.M.–9:00 P.M., Monday–Saturday; 11:00 A.M.–6:00 P.M., Sunday
Stores:
Aileen
American Tourister/Buxton
Aunt Mary's Yarns
Banister Shoes
Barbizon
Bass Shoes
Black & Decker
Book Warehouse
Boston Trader Kids
Bugle Boy Outlet
Cape Isle Knitters
Carter's Childrenswear
Columbia Sportswear Outlet
Corning/Revere
Crazy Horse
Dansk
Eddie Bauer
Famous Brands Housewares
Famous Footwear
Farah Factory Store
Farberware
Fieldcrest Cannon
Florsheim
Geoffrey Beene
Gitano
Great Outdoor Clothing
Helly-Hansen

Hush Puppies Factory Direct
JH Collectibles
Johnston & Murphy
Jones New York
Jordache
Kitchen Collection
Lands' End Outlet
Leather Loft
L'eggs/Hanes/Bali
London Fog
Natural Footgear
Newport Sportswear
Nickels Company Store
Old Mill Ladies Sportswear
OshKosh B'Gosh
Ozcan Sportswear
Paper Factory
Perfumania
Regal Outlet Store
Ribbon Outlet, Inc.
Royal Doulton
Russell
S & K Famous Brands
Socks Galore
Specials Exclusively by Levi's
Sports Factory
Stone Mountain Handbags
Swank
Sweatshirt Company
Toy Liquidators
Van Heusen
Wallet Works
Welcome Home
Westport Ltd./Westport Woman
Winona Knits
Credit Cards: Most stores accept major credit cards
Personal Checks: Most stores accept checks with driver's license and major credit card

Handicapped Accessible: Yes
Food: Food court in mall
Bus Tours: Yes
Notes or Attractions: EAA Air Adventure Museum across the highway

Racine

Western Publishing Outlet/The Boat House
2113 North Wisconsin Street

Directions: From I–94 take the Highway 20 exit 10 miles to Main Street, turning north. Travel 2 miles to Wisconsin Street and turn west. Outlet is 1 block farther.
Phone: (414) 631–1416
Hours: 9:00 A.M.–4:30 P.M., Monday–Friday; 8:00 A.M.–noon, Saturdays during October, November, December
Additional Savings: October through December
Credit Cards: No
Personal Checks: Yes, with driver's license
Handicapped Accessible: Yes
Food: 1–2 miles away
Bus Tours: Yes
Notes or Attractions: Near sandy beach and restored lakefront and across from a free zoo

Ripon

Fox River Glove Outlet Store
113 W. Fond Du Lac Street

Directions: Highway 23 to Ripon; just off town square in downtown Ripon
Phone: (414) 748–5845
Hours: 8:00 A.M.–8:00 P.M., Monday–Friday; 9:00 A.M.–5:00 P.M., Saturday; 10:00 A.M.–4:00 P.M., Sunday
Additional Savings: Sales from January through March and August through October

Credit Cards: MasterCard, Visa
Personal Checks: Yes, with identification
Handicapped Accessible: Yes
Food: Restaurants in downtown area several blocks away
Bus Tours: Yes

Stevens Point

Herrschners Factory Outlet
2800 Hoover Road

Directions: Highway 51 north to Highway 10 west exit; left (west) at first light 1 block to Country Club Road; continue 1 mile south to Hoover Road
Phone: (715) 341–8686
Hours: 9:00 A.M.–5:00 P.M., Monday–Saturday; 11:00 A.M.–4:00 P.M., Sunday
Additional Savings: Annual warehouse sale Wednesday through Saturday during third week in June
Credit Cards: MasterCard, Visa
Personal Checks: Yes, with identification
Handicapped Accessible: Yes
Food: 1 mile away
Bus Tours: Yes
Notes or Attractions: Factory tours with advance notice

West Bend

West Bend Outlet Mall
180 Island Avenue

Directions: Corner of Highway 33 and Island Avenue
Phone: (414) 334–3477
Hours: 9:30 A.M.–9:00 P.M., Monday–Friday; 9:30 A.M.–5:00 P.M., Saturday; 11:00 A.M.–5:00 P.M., Sunday
Additional Savings: Annual sale on Maxwell Street Day, first Wednesday of August

Stores: (Partial listing; not all stores are outlets)
Bass Shoes
The Cookie Jar Cookie Outlet
Full Size Fashions
Houseware Outlet
Little Red Shoe House
Paper Factory
Rainbow Fashions
Regal Outlet Store
Van Heusen
Credit Cards: Most stores accept major credit cards
Personal Checks: Yes, with identification
Handicapped Accessible: Yes, with a wheelchair available
Food: Food court in mall
Bus Tours: Yes
Notes or Attractions: Connected to downtown West Bend by a covered bridge over the Milwaukee River

Product Index

Athletic Apparel, Sportswear

Athletic/Sports Footwear

Books

Bridal

Candles

Christmas Decor

Mall Index

Outlet Index

MI: Birch Run, 105
WI: Kenosha, 179

Brass Factory Outlet
IL: Gurnee, 68
MI: Monroe, 110
OH: Milan, 165

Brass Town
MI: Holland, 107

The Brighter Side
WI: Kenosha, 176

Bristol County
WI: Kenosha, 176

Brooks Fashion Company Store
IL: Gurnee, 68

Brownberry Bakery Outlet
WI: Kenosha, 176

Brown Shoe Outlet
MN: Branch, 119
    Woodbury, 128

Bruce Alan Bags, Etc.
MI: Birch Run, 105
    West Branch, 113
MO: Branson, 132
    Osage Beach, 141

Bubbles and Scents Factory Outlet
MN: Chaska, 121
    Shakopee, 128

Bugle Boy Outlet
IL: Gurnee, 68
IN: Edinburgh, 83
    Fremont, 86
    Michigan City, 90
IA: Williamsburg, 99
MI: Birch Run, 103
    Holland, 107
    Kimball, 109
    Monroe, 110
    Traverse City, 112
MN: Branch, 119
    Woodbury, 128
MO: Branson, 132
    Sikeston, 143
    Wentzville, 144
OH: Milan, 165
WI: Oshkosh, 187

Burlington Coat Factory Warehouse
IN: Indianapolis, 87
MO: Wentzville, 144
OH: Columbus, 157
WI: Appleton, 172

Burlington Shoes
IL: Gurnee, 68

Burnham Glove Factory Outlet
IN: Michigan City, 88

Calvin Klein
WI: Kenosha, 179

Cambridge Dry Goods
WI: Kenosha, 179

WI: Kenosha, 176
    Oshkosh, 187

Casual Male Big and Tall
IL: Gurnee, 68
OH: Columbus, 159
WI: Kenosha, 176

Champion Hanes
IL: St. Charles, 74
IN: Fremont, 86
    Michigan City, 90
IA: Williamsburg, 99
MI: Birch Run, 103
    Kimball, 109
MO: Branson, 132
OH: Aurora, 147
    Milan, 165

Champs Outlet
IL: Gurnee, 68

Chaus
IN: Michigan City, 90
IA: Williamsburg, 99
MI: Birch Run, 105
MN: Medford, 124
MO: Osage Beach, 141
WI: Kenosha, 179

Chicago Records
IL: St. Charles, 75
WI: Kenosha, 176

Chico's
IL: Gurnee, 68
IN: Michigan City, 90

Children's Place
OH: Cincinnati, 153

China Plus
OH: Milan, 165

Cirage
IL: Gurnee, 68

Claires Clearance
IL: St. Charles, 75

Class Perfume
IL: Gurnee, 68

Clothes Outs
WI: Kenosha, 176

Clothestime
IL: Gurnee, 68
    Schaumburg, 76

Clothing by Farah
WI: Kenosha, 177

Coach
MI: West Branch, 113

Colours by Alexander Julian
IL: Gurnee, 68

Columbia Sportswear
MI: Birch Run, 103
WI: Oshkosh, 187

The Company Store
WI: Kenosha, 177

Shoe Sensation
OH: Cincinnati, 153
    Columbus, 156

Shoe Stop Outlet Store
IL: Fairview Heights, 65

Side-Out
IN: Michigan City, 91

Silkcorp
IL: Gurnee, 69

Simandl Coat Factory
IL: Cicero, 62

Sizes Unlimited
IN: Indianapolis, 87

Skyr
MI: Birch Run, 104

Smoler Brothers Outlet
IL: Chicago, 61

Sneakers 'n Cleats
MI: Birch Run, 104

Socks Galore/Socks Galore and More
IN: Edinburgh, 84
    Fremont, 86
    Michigan City, 91
IA: Williamsburg, 100
MI: Birch Run, 104
    Holland, 108
    Kimball, 109
    Monroe, 110
    Traverse City, 113

MN: Branch, 119
    Medford, 124
    Woodbury, 129
MO: Branson, 133
OH: Milan, 166
WI: Kenosha, 178
    Oshkosh, 188

Sony Factory Outlet Center
WI: Kenosha, 178

Specials Exclusively by Levi's
IL: Gurnee, 69
IN: Edinburgh, 84
    Michigan City, 91
MI: Birch Run, 104
    Kimball, 109
    Monroe, 110
    Traverse City, 113
MN: Woodbury, 129
WI: Oshkosh, 188

Spiegel Outlet
IL: Gurnee, 69

Sports Authority
IL: Gurnee, 69

Sports Factory
WI: Oshkosh, 188

Sportsland USA
MI: Birch Run, 104
    Holland, 108
    Monroe, 110

Sports Wearhouse
MI: Birch Run, 104